LONDON

LONDON
GOES TO SEA

*Restoring and Sailing
an Old Boat on a Budget*

PETER BAUMGARTNER

SHERIDAN HOUSE

First published 2004 by
Sheridan House Inc.
145 Palisade Street
Dobbs Ferry, NY 10522
www.sheridanhouse.com

Portions of the text first appeared as an article, "From LOON to LONDON," in the 2001 January and March issues of *Good Old Boat* magazine, in a slightly different form.

Portions of the text first appeared as an article "How to Run Aground" in the May 2002 issue of *SAIL Magazine,* in a slightly different form.

The quotations from the article "Hiking to Georges Bank," by Robert Buchsbaum, are used with the permission of *Sanctuary Magazine.*

The charts were drawn by Karen Baumgartner.
The sketch illustrations were drawn by Tyler Smithers and Karen Baumgartner.
The boat plan was drawn by Adam Koppel.

While all reasonable care has been taken in the publication
of this book, the publisher takes no responsibility for the use
of the methods or products described in the book.

Charts in the book are NOT to be used for navigation.
Use current NOAA charts corrected by Local Notice to Mariners.

Library of Congress Cataloging-in-Publication Data
Baumgartner, Peter J.
    London goes to sea : restoring and sailing an old boat on a budget /
Peter J. Baumgartner.
        p. cm.
    Includes bibliographical references.
    ISBN 1-57409-175-1 (pbk. : alk. paper)
    1. Boats and boating. 2. Boats and boating—Maintenance and repair.
3. Baumgartner, Peter J.—Travel. 4. London (Boat) I. Title.
GV775 .B33 2004
797.1'24—dc22   2003024613

Printed in the United States of America

ISBN   1-57409-175-1

Text design by Keata Brewer

Contents

Acknowledgments

This book is dedicated to Donald Pace, who left us suddenly long before his time was up.

I would like to thank my mother and father for their continued encouragement, Carolyn Marks for selling me LOON and talking to me about her, Paul Hailey for inspecting LOON and giving me the confidence to tackle the restoration, Darra Pace for being such a fan, Richard Tubman for always encouraging me to go sailing, Bruce Kulik for helping with the seasonal hauls, Kim Beckham for her bibliographical help, Mary Meltaus for coining the term "Old Reliable," Steve Loutrel for his expert advice, Andy Koppel for his editing help, and Gary Barna for his help with the boat. Peter Fifield showed me how to rig her, the way to Nantucket, and how to poach fish. Sam Lawson showed me LONDON and made sure I got her.

Two editors encouraged me to continue to write about sailing and boats: Karen Larson at *Good Old Boat* and Amy Ulrich at *SAIL* Magazine. Thank you.

Many members of the online Cape Dory newsgroup answered my questions, freely giving their advice and assistance, especially: Duncan Maio, Matt Cawthorne, Neil Gordon, Don Sargeant, Roald Horton, Scott, Don McLoughlin, Bob Miller, Giles Morris, Jerry Albright, Joe Brown, Tom, Lyn Heiges, Richard, Richard Gelfand, David Brownlee, Mike Thorpe, Jim Stull, Steve, Yves Feder, John Vigor, Geezer, Allen Evans, Ken Coit, Clay Stalker, Catherine Monaghan, Walt Bilofsky, and many more. George Dinwiddie, of the Alberg 30 site, was also a great help.

I would also like to thank the harbormasters of Rockport, Massachusetts for the lobsters and the fun; Captain Joe of the Florida

Keys; Captain "Bayfield" of Mystic, Connecticut; Captain Freddie of Biddeford Pool, Maine and the other lobstermen who helped pull me off the ledge; Bill and Dave of Earls Marina; the crews at Portland Yacht Services, Robinhood Marine, and Town River Marina; the Portsmouth, New Hampshire U.S. Coast Guard group, the New England Pilots Association, and the Cape Cod Canal Authority; the librarians of the Concord Free Public Library, Carlisle's Gleason Library, and the Phillips Library of the Peabody Essex Museum who helped so much with the research and retrieval of scores of books; and Charlene Bickford at George Washington University for checking some of my history.

But most of all I want to thank my wife Nancy and my daughters for their continual support and encouragement.

With the first dipping of the oars the theme of the introduction came to me.

—Gustav Mahler

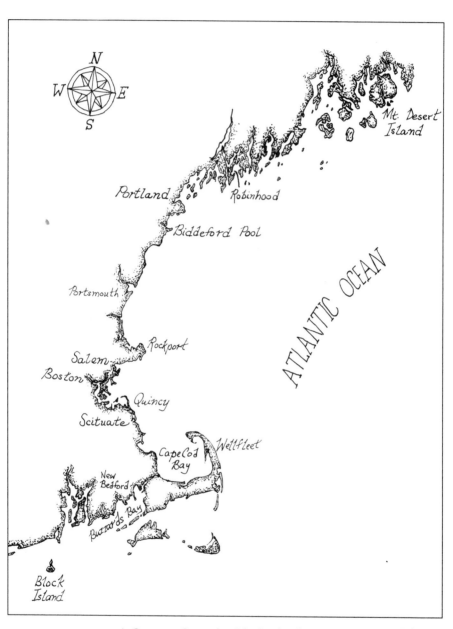

LONDON's Cruising Ground—Block Island to Mt. Desert

Introduction

We roll into the marina parking lot late in the morning with sailing gear stacked high in the back of the station wagon. Low gray clouds race across the harbor. My boat is tethered to her mooring in the choppy water. She pulls one way and then the other. The gusty wind shakes her like a fish hooked but still fighting to be free—to sail, to tack, and then to surge ahead with her jib straining for hours without end, spray flying over the bow, before the cry "Ready about! Hard a lee!" brings her across to the new heading with a bang of the boom against the mainsheet. It is not to be. At least not yet. We will spend time ashore in New Bedford and do our sailing later. It looks like rain. It is a little too rough.

In New Bedford, under the same gray clouds racing across the sky, we come upon a group in the street, two men and three women. They surround a National Park tour guide, who looks us over, sees our shorts, our sandals, and invites us to join them. We stand with them on the hard cobble sidewalk and listen. I see the trees heave in the wind. I hear the words "Moby Dick" blown from her lips. Moby Dick is everywhere in New Bedford. It is about all that's left.

New Bedford was prosperous when whale oil was the oil. It brought wealth to the owners of whaling ships. Downtown was full of banks and financial institutions. Quaker merchants grew rich, but lived simply.

Our guide takes us into the Seamen's Bethel. She explains that "Bethel" is a word with a Hebrew derivation, *Beth* meaning house and *El* meaning god: *House of God*. The chapel was built with the contributions of concerned merchants to improve the character and lives of the seamen serving on their whaling ships. In the classic

Melville novel *Moby Dick*, before Ishmael sets off on his voyage, he visits the "Whaleman's Chapel," where the pulpit is high and shaped like the bow of a ship. We are in that chapel. It is August. The sultry light pours through the tall, many-paned, wood-framed windows and flows across the planked floor. Outside the wind whips the trees, one way and then the other. Our guide is speaking.

> A marathon reading of *Moby Dick* is held every January across the street at the Whaling Museum. The chapter about Father Mapple's sermon is read here, then everyone goes back across the street to the Whaling Museum to complete the reading. It takes twenty-four hours to read the book; each volunteer reads for about ten minutes. You can sign up across the street. There's a whaling dinner and a breakfast. The reading always starts at noon on January 3, the day Herman Melville shipped out on a whaler from New Bedford. The ship was the ACUSHNET, the year 1841.

Sitting on the hard pews in the Seamen's Bethel, we are surrounded by names on cenotaphs, memorial lists of lost men, their bodies in the sea. In *Moby Dick*, Melville described the scene here and the cenotaphs in a chapter titled "The Chapel":

> A muffled silence reigned, only broken at times by the shrieks of the storm. Each silent worshipper seemed purposely sitting apart from the other, as if silent grief were insular and incommunicable. The chaplain had not yet arrived; and yet there these silent islands of men and women sat steadfastly eyeing several marble tablets, with black borders, masoned into the wall on each side of the pulpit.

The memorial dates run from the early days of New Bedford up to the present time. One of the last names on the list marks a loss I remember. In January 1999 the CAPE FEAR was dragging for clams some 20 miles south of Cuttyhunk. On her way back to New Bedford she swamped and then sank near the entrance to Buzzards Bay in the roar of an approaching winter gale. She was raised from the bottom the following summer by a crane mounted on a barge. One morning the wreck of the CAPE FEAR appeared in the lee of West Island with a tugboat and the crane barge, to which she was tethered with giant, black steel cables. The wreck remained there for a week or two. A floating oil boom surrounded the little fleet to contain oil spills. I would sail by, making my usual way between my mooring and the open summer waters of Buzzards Bay. The CAPE FEAR's cabintop was smashed in and slimy, a frightening sight. Men were lost when she went down. Names for the cenotaph. A chill afloat.

The CAPE FEAR reminds me that there is no comparison between the sea conditions for coastal sailors like myself, who go out when they want to and stay in port when they don't, and those experienced by fishermen and others who work on the water, who go to sea all year, through the seasons of hardship and storms.

No yachtsmen appear on the walls of the Seamen's Bethel in New Bedford and yet, in some fashion, the danger experienced by professional mariners becomes part of the lore, part of the background of man against nature. It adds excitement to the sport of sailing, even if today we chose not to set sail on a breezy afternoon with threatening showers while they are out on George Bank, dragging the ever deep.

So, on the good days, I am drawn to the water.

When I was about eleven, I lived in England, attended a boy's school named St. Christopher's, and wore the insulting uniform of shorts, striped tie, and jacket. The school's masters soon discovered not only that I could not sing, but that I would in my enthusiasm to be heard ruin the clear, high sound of the preadolescent boy's choir with my off-key atonal voice. I was removed from the chorus and grouped with a few other boys. There would be no singing for us. The Latin master began to teach us a poem we would recite to our families. The poem, "Sea Fever," published in 1902 by John Masefield, set my course out to sea. To this day I hear its lines resonating from the dark rafters of the St. Christopher's school gymnasium.

I must down to the seas again, to the lonely sea and the sky,
And all I ask is a tall ship and a star to steer her by,
And the wheel's kick and the wind's song and the white sail's shaking,
And a grey mist on the sea's face and a grey dawn breaking.

I needed a boat.

I would have many small boats along the way, rowboats, canoes, kayaks, and dinghies, boats which teased me with the sensation of floating and voyage but were somehow unsatisfying. Then I saw an old cruising sailboat in someone's backyard—a sailboat I knew at first sight was my boat—an apparent wreck of a boat I would attempt to float. She was named LOON.

My first boat was a wooden rowboat on the coast of Maine. I was a teenager. My older cousin Bryon taught me to row from our cold water cove to the tidal ledges a mile or more out. We would ride the small swells as they broke between the rocks and ledges, scramble over the slippery rockweed, and land on those islands we could get a grip on.

I loved the cool salty scent of the open ocean on a warm day, the smell that lies close to the surface of the rolling swell, the smell you can almost see as a delicate white mist just above the water's surface.

At home in New Jersey, my father bought a small fiberglass dinghy we could trailer, sail, and row. We sailed this dinghy across Wellfleet Harbor on summer vacation. In the cold off-season, he and I fished from it for succulent winter flounder along the protected bays of the Jersey shore. I best remember sailing this boat across a New Jersey lake on a gusty summer day and, by refusing to let up on the mainsheet, capsizing it and dumping my mother into the water repeatedly with the impunity of a son much loved.

"Are you doing this on purpose?"

"No, Mom."

At twenty-two I built my first boat. It was a Cambridge River punt. I built it with Ian, a burly red-headed Canadian Scots lumberman, my girlfriend's father, during the time I lived with them in the basement of their house on Vancouver Island, British Columbia. The punt had a freeboard of about 9 inches. It was remarkably unsuited for the waters of the Strait of Juan de Fuca, which separates Vancouver Island from Washington State's Olympic Peninsula to the south.

The Strait began at the bottom of their yard, just behind a lush 12-foot hedge. I named this new punt the GREAT BLUE HERON, a.k.a. GBH, and painted her a glossy blue, too bright to resemble the great bird itself. Ian was as helpful as he could be while I struggled with her construction. It was he who found the yellow cedar for her curved thwarts after I had snapped my supply of Douglas fir with impatient eagerness to make wood bend.

I launched her with a big push and hopped in, and water poured over her thwarts and I rolled over into the icy waters of the Strait. I went all the way in—over and under. The first thing I saw when I stood waist-deep among the little waves of the cove, coughing and spitting, wiping my eyes and shaking the water off, was Donna laughing hysterically from the rocky, log-strewn beach. Dripping and humiliated I dragged the boat out of the freezing water, chased Donna back to the house, changed my clothes, and came back down to the shore to try again. I learned to stay low and balance my weight. I would not roll over again.

I used GBH to fish for rock bass among the kelp beds, and on calm days I rowed out into the Strait to look back at the fir hills of Vancouver Island. When I left the island I left GBH behind for the use of Ian's clan. Donna's nephews would row GBH out among the rocks and fish as I had done, while she watched from the beach.

Back in New Hampshire, my sister's boyfriend introduced me to canoe camping. You can carry a lot of gear in a canoe. On our first trip, Bill and my sister Karen packed live lobsters, all the ingredients to make fresh blueberry ice cream, and an ice cream maker into two canoes for an evening feast on a small, round island in the Connecticut River. The next summer six of us paddled two canoes and a kayak north from near Hearst, Ontario on the Trans-Canada Highway, down one river and then another until we turned east on the Albany River and then out into James Bay. We were in those boats for more than ten days, sleeping on the sandy riverbanks at night, paddling all day. By the time we approached James Bay, the Albany River was a mile wide and shallow. After our last day of paddling and dragging the boats across the sandy shoals, we pitched our tents on property of the Hudson's Bay trading post at Fort Albany.

After that trip I wanted a kayak of my own. I now knew how much easier it was to paddle a kayak against the wind than a canoe, and that kayaks were more stable and safer. You could take them out on salt water, where I wanted to be. At the time I was reading *The Starship and the Canoe*, a book about seagoing kayaks[1]. From this book I also learned about *The Bark Canoes and the Skin Boats of North America*, the Smithsonian's classic text on traditional native American boat construction.

I built a two-man kayak in the basement of my house over the course of one winter. A Folbot, it came as a kit. In the evenings I would get a fire going in the basement fireplace and then, with the snow swirling around outside, cut and glue the pieces of the inner frame together. I loved the look of that boat when she was all frame. Her lines were crisp and alluring. I even delayed putting on the skin, which would hide the skeleton. My boat resembled the black-and-white line drawing of a kayak from Kodiak Island, Alaska in my Smithsonian book, although the bow of my boat was a simple one, without the curious bifid decoration found on the native design. The work moved outside in the spring. I covered the frame with a green rubber skin and got her ready to go.

North Bridge in Concord, Massachusetts is a few miles from home. My friend John D. and I set off in June from just above the bridge to paddle down the Concord River and then the Merrimack to reach the ocean. It took us two days. At the end of the first day we car-portaged around the rapids near the city of Lowell and spent the night at the Lowell Hilton. We left the kayak in the hotel's parking lot. The next morning we put in again and ran the remainder of the Merrimack down to Newburyport Harbor. At the end of the day we climbed out near the old granite Custom House in the brackish tidal waters of historic Newburyport.

Later that summer, while paddling the kayak through the salt marshes and harbors off Ipswich, Massachusetts, I began to dwell on cruising sailboats. I remember moving through an anchorage off the Ipswich Yacht Club with John L. We stopped every few strokes to admire the traditional lines of the boats. John said he would like to get an old, single-sailed catboat, that these were the old workboats of New England—good family boats.

Coastal kayaking was a step toward sailing. Kayaking gave me a chance to experience the currents and wind close at hand. To get a better feel for the sea. Inevitably, bigger boats appeared on my horizon, boats with long, heavy keels, sails, and small diesel engines. Boats that could take me on extended self-propelled trips up and down the coast.

The kayak I built was 17 feet long; the sailboat I would eventually buy was 27 feet. A difference of 10 feet in length may not sound like much until you consider the weight. The kayak weighs 75 pounds; the sailboat weighs a hundred times that—7,500 pounds. They are worlds apart. I can live on the sailboat for weeks at a time and travel hundreds of miles in real comfort. I have fallen asleep at the tiller of my sailboat. She just keeps on sailing. If I fell asleep in my kayak I would lose my paddle.

I became obsessed with sailing and everything that went along with it: sail handling, seamanship, and navigation; physics, oceanography, astronomy, and fluid mechanics; the vagaries of wind, weather, and the atmosphere; electronics and radio; fiberglass repair, diesel mechanics, wiring, plumbing, woodworking, and metalwork; knots and rigging; the rules of the road; first aid, safety measures, and emergency survival procedures; diet and nutrition, cooking, and food storage; waste management and environmental considerations; the record left by others who have sailed—a great maritime literature to be explored, contemporary and historical, narrative and practical; the delight of observing and identifying all the categories of pelagic life—fishes, birds, whales, dolphins, crustaceans, and invertebrates; and finally the community of other sail-boats with other sailors at their tillers with genoas aloft, mainsails trimmed just so, and a gleam in their eyes.

This great variety of learning and experience is a key to the fascination. I have been told that many sailors live with the continual inevitability of the unexpected. I certainly do. Things happen. Things go wrong. Mistakes bring on problems, and even if no mistakes in technique are made, adventures arise out of equipment malfunction and the vagaries and variations of weather and currents. Being afloat is a fluid state. Change is inevitable—expected.

This book is about my experience of repairing and improving an old sailboat, of getting and being afloat, of the people I met, the wonder, the adventures, the learning. It is in many ways a book of mistakes that I managed not to avoid, an archaeology of errors in seamanship and boat handling in the face of those constant inquisitors—the sea, the wind, and the self. The cruising sailboat is a vehicle of exploration, a vehicle of learning, a vehicle of challenge.

Carlisle, Massachusetts
December 11, 2002

1

LOON Alone

Late in the evening the smell of diesel exhaust settles onto the ground as the big truck pulls away. Metal stands press into her fiberglass flanks below the painted waterline. The wood blocks under LOON's keel begin to settle into the lawn. They press the blades of grass flat against the earth. The patch of lawn under these blocks will soon be dead, killed by the weight of the boat above, crushed and suffocated as if by the deep of the sea itself.

It took all summer for the engine to be repaired, and it was August before the boat was ready, too late in the season for a launch. At the back of the boatyard one dry season had become another until time itself seemed to have stopped. There was only the fence, the gravel, and the sky itself.

And now this. Two years after that first missed season, only to be moved further away from the water, out of the boatyard and away from the company of other hulls, away from the salt air into a limbo here at the corner of this flat yard, under these two trees. The air seems so hot. The companionway hatch has begun to buckle under the weight of the unstepped mast. A leaf floats through the air and settles on the cockpit floor. Lights in the house across the yard come on. A man and a woman come out of the house and walk around the hull. The man reaches out and brushes the hull with the tips of his fingers. Just the once. The woman stands a bit further back. They are quiet and soon go away. The long wait has begun. It feels very dry. It is beginning to get dark.

A boat out of water is a dead thing, a beached whale. So massive, so still. Underwater parts naked and visible. Something to be examined and clambered over, poked and prodded, something a little less alive, a little drier every day.

2

From LOON to LONDON

Early in the summer of 1998 I find her in Quincy, Massachusetts, a historic New England town along the southern edge of Boston Harbor. She is uncovered. Up on her stands along the back edge of the yard, under a pair of trees, LOON—a 27-foot Cape Dory sailboat with an 8 hp single-cylinder diesel engine, hull number 35, built in 1977—is barely breathing. She has been out of the water for ten years. Her mast lies atop the cabin. Stains streak her sides. Mice and birds have been in the mast. The halyards, strewn every which way, are green and rotting. The cockpit is full of leaves and stained from their decay. The teak is many colors—black, gray, green. Peeling duct tape covers the holes where her instruments must have been. Sam, the broker, has arrived before me and is dumping leaves out of the cockpit. He apologizes for the condition of the boat.

"I'm sorry. I haven't seen her for years."

I say nothing. She has everything I want—standing room in the cabin, an inboard diesel, a full keel—and she is probably cheap. It takes all summer to negotiate the price down to what I think she is worth. I have had a cash windfall of $10,000 and I intend to spend all of it on a boat. I agree to buy her for $10,500.

My wife Nancy and I pace around our yard looking for a place to put the boat. We live about 20 miles from the ocean, northwest of Boston, on about two acres of land, but most of our property is wetland; dry, level ground is scarce. We settle on a spot between the

garage and the street. Before LOON arrives I use my chain saw to remove a few trees. Nancy likes this spot because she will not be able
to see the boat from the house.

With a shovel and a rake I smooth and pack the ground to make
a large flat surface. Thirty feet away a shed runs along one side of
the garage. I will use the shed as my workshop and for the storage
of boat stuff. LOON is coming with plenty of gear. If you buy an old
boat from someone who is getting out of sailing, you tend to get the
lot—old barbecues, fire extinguishers, awnings, dodgers, old charts,
and the like. I clean up the shed and organize my tools. Power and
water are close by. When the tractor trailer arrives, I am ready. The
driver is a Quincy fireman, part-time boat hauler.

"What a great spot for a boat!"

Paul backs the trailer in, uses the padded hydraulic arms to lower
the boat onto some huge beams he's brought, and braces her with
adjustable metal tripod stands before pulling the trailer out from underneath. I get a ladder and Paul climbs up into the cockpit to pour
a bucket of water and see how it will drain. He adjusts the angle of
her pitch, I write a check, and he is gone. I stand in the street for a
long time just staring at her. It is Columbus Day, 1998.

As it happens we are having a party that evening. A group of
friends come outside in the twilight, glasses of wine and beer in
hand, to look her over. There is a polite silence after my excited bab-
ble about the boat. I look up and see what they see—the stains, the
musty smell, rotten lines trailing off the stern, rusty rigging strewn
about, three or four tons of junk. John looks at me for a moment
before speaking, as if considering his words.

"You've got your work cut out for you."

I feel the first twinge of doubt.

The next morning I begin by taking absolutely everything off the
boat—from the boom to the anchors, flares to cushions, life jackets
to silverware. It all lands on the ground and is either cleaned and
stored in the shed or put in a pile for a trip to the town dump. I pick
up two docklines, climb up into the trees near the boat, and tightly
string one line above the deck across her bow and the other equally

high across her stern. I run additional lines from the head and tail of her mast over the two overhead lines.

I go into the house and find my thirteen-year-old daughter. We each grab a line and hoist the mast up into the air, pull it out along the cross lines so it hangs parallel to the boat, and lower it to the ground. My daughter runs back into the house. With the mast off the boat I have more room to move about, and I begin to clean—first with a broom and a shop vacuum and then with a hose and a scrub brush. I clean and scrub all day. And the next. And the weekend after that.

The weather remains mild through November, and I work on her whenever I have free time. During this period I sleep well and awake stiff but purposeful. Scrubbing dirty and stained fiberglass is satisfying work. You get to see real progress. My dog lies near the boat chewing an endless series of sticks into chips and watching me go up and down the ladder.

I find that for cleaning the fiberglass above the waterline, it is best first to wash off the gross dirt by scrubbing with a solution made up of a cup of bleach and some TSP in a bucket of water. I use a scrub brush and a scrub pad and wear rubber gloves. I then hose the surface off and apply a powerful acidic fiberglass cleaner according to the manufacturer's directions. I use a natural bristle brush to apply the cleaner, as it will soften and dissolve the artificial bristles of a paintbrush. You must wear gloves and eye protection and avoid breathing the fumes. It is a good idea to keep a hose nearby to flush your skin with water in case of any splashes. I sometimes help the cleaning process along by gently and carefully scrubbing the surface I have painted with the cleaner with a wet scrub pad. The manufacturer does not recommend this, but I find it effective. I finish up with a good water flush of the area, and a further polish of any remaining stains with bleach and TSP again. A little cleanser on a scrub pad can really help at this point. No stains will stand up to this treatment. The fiberglass begins to gleam again. I rub the name LOON off the stern with cleanser and scrub pads and remove the last paint spots with very fine, wet sandpaper.

There is a lot of teak on a Cape Dory. I begin by removing all the hardware—cleats, snaps for the dodger, plates, etc.—and put each set with fasteners into a separate plastic bag and store them in the shed. I scrub the teak, again with that combination of bleach and TSP, using what has become my favorite scrub pad. After the wood is dry, I use my power orbital finishing sander to sand it all down. A number of the teak plugs along the toerails are extruded or broken. These I remove and replace with new teak plugs, which I set in place with two-part marine glue and then sand flush. I hand sand all the teak with fine sandpaper, vacuum, and wipe all the dust away. By the time the weather finally begins to turn colder, I have a couple of coats of semi-gloss on all the teak and the exterior fiberglass is clean.

One Sunday I stop work and sit on the cabintop in the warm afternoon sun. I can see over the garage roof to the wet meadow beyond where the tall grass waves in the breeze. I watch the grass wave and imagine myself at sea. I am very happy. It is ridiculous. So far all the work has been cosmetic—I have not even started on the boat's systems. Yet I continue to sit in the sun, admire my boat, and daydream.

Her transom is now a blank. Once I had LOON I wanted to rename her. In naming something we give it a power or quality. The ancient Romans believed in something like that. In their old religion there were many powers in the spirit world, but by naming them the power could be manifest, channeled to their will. This naming became a rite, a ritual, to invoke the power. The name I would give my new boat would also in some way define her, carry some message. I thought her name should be an echo of something I loved. Something female, boat forms being more like women than men.

At first I thought I would follow in my father-in-law's footsteps and give her a name derived from my daughters' names. His daughters were Darra and Nancy, and their wooden cabin cruiser, kept along the southern shore of Long Island, was named the DARNAN. My own daughters, so independent and beautiful, are Kate and Laura.

Kate is a good name. Good and strong, like Kate herself. I knew this name would keep me safe. There is something to that. A boat name is in some fashion a symbol of your protection, a marker of what keeps you safe. I know I can count on Kate. When she was small, Kate gave me a coffee mug that had on opposite sides the fore and aft views of a huge dog, with a little pup at its feet. The pup has one black eye. "Don't mess with My Dad!" is printed around the base of the mug.

I also thought about naming her after my youngest daughter. I had seen at least one other boat named after her, when I was crewing for my friend Steve, bringing his big, wooden Concordia yawl LACERTA down from Maine. That is a beautiful boat. Steve, being an MIT engineering sort, has everything aboard done so perfectly. She sails like a solid dream. The week I spent on her in late August there was a hurricane passing by way off the coast. When big storms pass by like that, although the weather remains fine, with a deep blue sky and perhaps a bit of a long swell, things become unstable. Instability means wind, likely more than forecast, and this is what we got. LACERTA heeled over to the rails and went, but being wooden and substantial she was wonderfully stable. She drove on at 7 or 8 knots. We wove through the sparkling air past the coastal islets and around Port Clyde, where we were lucky enough to pass the little ferry LAURA B. on her way out to Monhegan Island. Laura B. is my other daughter. She too would protect.

I looked up at the boat transom again. LOON. A flighty, teasing sound. Loon, a bird who speaks loudly, from afar, with a warbled call. The poet Celia Thaxter knew the loons around the Isles of Shoals. In her wonderful book *Among the Isles of Shoals* (1873), Thaxter describes talking with the birds in their own tongue:

> At one time the loon language was so familiar that I could always summon a considerable flock by going down to the water and assuming the neighborly and conversational tone which they generally use: after calling a few minutes, first a far off voice responded, then other voices answered him, and when this was kept up a while, half a dozen birds would come sailing in.[2]

I hear the bird's call in the name itself. It makes me think of Canada, vast empty spaces, spruces, and clear cold lakes. I look at the four black letters across her stern L-O-O-N and see a new name. I only need to add two letters. Perhaps this is a change small enough to avoid the wrath of Neptune and the curse known to sailors, the curse of renaming a boat.

London. I say the word slowly. It has a bass resonance. Two syllables, each ending in the low vibrato of the *n*. A word of substance. Ancient and lasting. I see the city and the swirling brown surface of the Thames from the footbridge at Charing Cross. I smell the acrid scent of burning coal on a December afternoon.

On a dark, midwinter afternoon I enter a London park. The air is damp. The sounds of the city traffic recede behind my feet crunching over the loose stone path. I hurry past the wet stone monument where the carved inscription of a phrase tossed off in cleverness some three or four hundred years ago still resonates, "When a man is tired of London, he is tired of life" and leave the park behind at the black iron gate. My footsteps echo with the others hurrying through the hard narrow streets of St. James toward the end of the day. My route twists and turns, until as I approach the theater, I look ahead.

Nancy is waiting off to one side. Behind me the sun suddenly drops below the black clouds into a band of clear sky right near the horizon. The bright light flows like liquid gold across the white pillars and at the entrance of the theater in front of me—dazzling and rich in the wet.

Even here in the midst of the city, protected by all these buildings, you can feel the ocean weather from the Atlantic some 60 miles to the west where it strikes the edges of Europe. Black clouds rush by overhead.

We press ourselves into the crowd of dark clothing and conversation. Behind us, outside the lobby doors, with their small panes of thick, dim glass, the sun, just as quickly as it appeared, vanishes. It will soon be dark. The lights along Haymarket begin to come on. After the play Nancy and I will eat at a small place along the Brompton Road and then walk home.

London. She will be called LONDON.

3

LONDON's Waterworks

I begin the work on the boat's plumbing, learning as I go. Although I have been sailing for years, I have never done any boat maintenance, much less replaced whole systems. I do not even have a complete idea of how they all work—water, electric, diesel and prop, the head. Fortunately there are a number of excellent books to read (see Chapter 19), and I have the good fortune to have chosen a boat that has attracted an active Internet newsgroup to which I can turn for help. I often receive several answers to the questions I post on the newsgroup by the very next day. Even with the manufacturer out of business, Cape Dorys command a lot of loyalty and pride[3].

I start my plumbing projects by pulling out all the freshwater, cockpit drain and head hoses. I attach a cutting disk to my handheld power tool. With it I cut the heavy, wire-reinforced hoses, carefully slicing each hose lengthwise along the pipe it is attached to without scoring the underlying fitting. I wear heavy leather gloves and eye protection during this process.

Cape Dorys are fitted with bronze, tapered plug-style seacocks. They are large, heavy, and impressive. The one that sits in the back of my head compartment looks like it belongs on a North Sea oil rig. Every single one of the six seacocks on the boat is frozen in the open position. Dealing with frozen seacocks is a frequent topic on the Cape Dory bulletin board. I have read about the different methods for getting the tapered plug out of the cylinder it has been embracing for the last ten or so years. The recommended approach is to apply penetrating oil, back the nut out to the end of the threaded stem (to avoid damaging the thread), and then tap the nut, protected with a scrap of wood, with a hammer. I find a heavy hammer helps. I use a brake puller where I have the room. It allows me to apply pressure and pop the tapered plugs out without any impact.

From the bulletin board I learn about an $11 "radiator spud wrench" I can get from a local hardware chain. From the outside of the boat I insert the spud wrench into a through-hull so it can engage the little bronze tabs on the inside of the pipe, tighten a pipe wrench on the square end for leverage, and turn. The through-hull should then unscrew. Once that is done, it is simple to remove the seacock itself.

I soon have all but two of the through-hulls and seacocks out of the boat, polished, and regreased. The tabs in both of the remaining seacocks' through-hulls break off as I try to unscrew them with the spud wrench. They are frozen in place. These last two are on the cockpit drains. Water running out of the uncovered boat for the last ten years has left them badly corroded. They are incredibly inconvenient to reach. I either have to kneel and reach around the engine, lie on the engine and reach down, or hang upside down in the cockpit locker. I lose a lot of time with these two. It is cold, so maybe I have slowed down as well, but it seems for a couple of weeks I am walking back and forth to the boat with different tools and pry bars and hammers, even some gadgets I made. Nothing seems to work.

The seacock on the port side finally yields its plug with a pop—to a long soak in penetrating oil and a blow from a padded but definitely annoyed sledgehammer. The starboard cockpit drain seacock will not yield. Finally on a cold day I sit down on a milk crate under the boat and begin to cut the through-hull with the high-speed cutting tool. Little sparks fly around my hands. After several cutter bits and considerable patience I am able to cut off the outer flanged portion of the through-hull and then knock the remainder up into the boat. I clean up the hole in the fiberglass hull, make a new tapered backing plate, coat it and the hole with epoxy, and buy and then install a new through-hull and seacock. I now have six working seacocks.

To overhaul the freshwater system I remove the plastic tank from the boat, clean it with a diluted bleach and water mixture, flush with fresh water, refill the tank with a baking soda mixture, and then flush again. I run a new water hose from the tank to the sink in the galley, add a new stainless steel deck fill for water on the starboard side of the bow, and run the fill hose into an opening I cut in the water tank and fit with a barbed tank fitting. I remove the old hand pump faucet and replace it with a simple spout and a new foot pump near the sink. The pump forces the fresh water through a 1-micron filter and out the spout into the sink.

On a day when there is a strong breeze blowing, I remove the old waste holding tank. I also remove and discard some other bits of hose and plumbing that are ruined and then wash the whole head and tank area with the TSP and bleach solution. Then I take a hot shower.

To make the waste system compliant, I route everything from the head to the holding tank. A 1½-inch exit hose runs from the holding tank to a Y-valve, which allows waste to be pumped overboard or into the holding tank, later to be vacuumed up through a deck port. I have trouble finding a holding tank that will fit with all its plumbing under the port forward berth. I eventually buy a polyethylene tank on which I can install the fittings where I need them. I use a hole-cutter on my electric drill to make the opening in the tank and then fasten the fittings in place with adhesive. Once this is done I remove the manual waste pump and disassemble, clean, and rebuild it before reinstalling it in the boat.

Before buying the boat I had it inspected. And for the most part, because of this survey I know her problems and strengths. On those dark days when things are not going well, when the loosening of a single frozen nut has stopped all progress, I can comfort myself with the firm knowledge that I possess a sturdy hull, or an intact and serviceable mainsail. I consider the money we paid for the survey one of the best possible investments.

A few days after the survey was completed, I received a written report on the condition of the boat. There were six or seven pages of commentary and another six or seven detailing the boat's specifications and equipment. The surveyor made a number of recommendations, which I intend to go through one by one, but the Yanmar diesel engine was thought to be in excellent condition. It had been completely rebuilt before the boat was laid up. I paid a small fee to have a second company that specializes in marine diesel repair come and try to start the engine while the marine surveyor was present. The mechanic connected the engine to a clean fuel tank, a cooling water source, and a working battery. The engine started right up and was run for about fifteen minutes. Everyone seemed relieved.

I replace all the engine's cooling hoses and rubber fuel lines and add a new seawater filter. I also add a new fuel filter with a water separator. I have been told to drain the old fuel out of the tank and get it cleaned.

After I pump the old diesel out of the tank I can see an amazing amount of crud and growth within. It looks more like the bottom of some dark primeval tide pool than a tank. Is that a trilobite?

I take the tank out of the boat, put it in the back of my old VW van, and drive to the local body shop hoping they can clean it. The two brothers who run the body shop and I take turns peering into the tank. The verdict is to buy a new tank. Again, as with the waste tank, it is hard to find a new tank of the correct proportions. I eventually find one only slightly larger and spend a pleasant weekend hanging upside down in the cockpit, a power jigsaw in hand, enlarging the fuel tank enclosure and rearranging the mounts so I can install it.

There are only four more things left to do in the bilge. Then I can stand up.

The old grounding plate had been painted over, so when Colin, my teenage nephew, is visiting we replace it and reattach the ground and lightning wires. I also get him to climb inside the cockpit locker to remove and replace two hose clamps around the stuffing box hose. It is an awkward position even for him, a lanky and flexible teen, but a handheld power screwdriver makes the job easier.

The little paddle wheel for the knot meter is thick with years of paint. I take it out of the boat, disassemble it, clean and grease it, and put it back. I add an automatic electric bilge pump and run a new bilge hose to a nylon through-hull I install above the waterline in the stern.

It is spring. The weather is getting warmer. My friend Rich calls on the phone to ask when I will launch the boat. I have no idea, but by the end of our call the launch is set for May. Having a launch date focuses me on what needs to get done. I organize my priorities.

During the winter I had measured the three old rotting rope and wire halyards and ordered ³/₈-inch line to replace them. I now splice thimble eyes into these lines using a splicing kit. Since I have never done this before and do not trust my splices, I take one of the new halyards outside and wrap one end around a tree and hook the other end to a come-along-style winch, which I fasten to another tree. I give it a good long tug with the winch. Convinced my splices will hold, I reeve the three new halyards through the mast.

Although we had not been able to get any electricity flowing during the inspection, because the positive wire to the fuse panel was broken, the work needed on the electrical system is straightforward once I replace the positive cable. I read how to use a volt/ohm meter to test for continuity and current flow. Then I check out all the circuits. All the connections are cleaned and resoldered. I buy new battery boxes and new batteries to go in them.

The navigation lights are all out. One by one I take them apart, clean them, replace the water seals, resolder the connections, and polish their metal exterior surfaces with the high-speed tool. I put new ends on the VHF coaxial cable that runs through the mast and install a new radio antenna (the insulator of the old antenna disintegrated in my hands). At the same time I install an anchor light at the masthead and run new wires to it through the mast. The combination deck and steaming light on the mast is rotten. I replace it with a new unit. I stock the electrical toolbox with spare bulbs, connectors, and fuses. My sister and her daughter Hannah help polish the mast. We are almost ready to go.

I need to get the mast off the ground, 10 feet up in the air, and onto the top of the boat before the truck can take us to the launch site. Although a friend from the Cape Dory newsgroup calculates the weight of my mast at slightly less than 100 pounds, it feels surprisingly heavy. My daughter and I may have been able to get it off the boat and down onto the ground, but there is no way we can get it back up onto the deck by ourselves, so one evening after work my friends Bruce, Mary, and Mary's husband Josiah come by to help. I have the head of the mast rigged up with a couple of blocks to the lines overhead, but I do not own enough blocks for the base end as well; at that end I just throw a few loops around the overhead line and then the base of the mast for extra purchase. The mast head lifts up onto the boat easily, but the foot of the mast we only get back up on deck with determination, many hands, and a few lucky heaves.

I have a photograph I took of LONDON the evening before the truck came to pick her up for the launch. She is sitting in the soft green light of the spring woods. Her topsides are again an almost pearly white, her boot stripe a sharp glossy red line above the flat tropical blue of her antifouling paint. I feel she may never look as clean and shiny as she does at this instant.

4

LONDON's Launch

On May 18, 1999, on the banks of the Town River in Quincy, I face my moment of truth. I spray LONDON's bow with an English ale and say a few words of blessing. I have challenged the Maritime Fates by renaming the boat LONDON. This is bad luck. I need to make amends. Bass Ale seems appropriate.

The truck driver, crane operator, and crew grin. I pass around the rest of the beer. The crane that steps the mast in the marina parking lot is a retired telephone truck. The crew string the stays and shrouds and help me with the fastenings. Incredibly, I have all the pieces we need to hold the mast up. We get off the boat and pull the ladder away. The truck backs LONDON toward the ramp that runs into the water.

She slips into the sea after eleven years of navigating backyards and boatyards. As the water begins to lap at her hull, my big question is whether or not she will float. Other questions follow. Will the mast stay up? Are there leaks? How will she sail? Did I tighten the hose clamps? Did I use enough bedding compound? Is this a huge mistake? Whatever made me think I could buy a neglected boat and recommission her? Am I completely crazy?

LONDON's hull is completely wet. For these first moments at least, she floats. I hop on board and look below. Water runs in through the stern tube in a steady stream, but after perhaps an hour this settles down to a steady drip—one that I, the batteries, and the new automatic bilge pump can live with for the summer. LONDON is tied to the dock. I feel the new sensation of her moving underfoot as I knock around below looking for leaks. Other than the stuffing box, not a drop!

This will be the first time I have seen the boat "put together," with her mast up and running rigging in place. I am not sure what will go where, but that evening my friend Pete comes down to the dock to help. We get the boom and the mainsail rigged and run the engine for a while. I leave the boat tied to the dock, stowing supplies and getting everything shipshape. It is a warm, still evening.

The slip I rented for these two weeks of commissioning is near the head of the Town River. It is away from the open waters of Boston Harbor and sheltered; but this evening you can smell the ocean a mile or so away. Our side of the river is densely developed. Just off a busy highway, the narrow drive into the marina passes between a muffler shop and a body shop, past an expanse of asphalt with boats and cars in various stages of rebuild. Four huge green oil tanks overshadow the eastern end of the marina shoreline, but the view across the river is to a protected natural area. Over there it looks wild and green with open marsh and scrub trees.

The next day Rich meets me at the dock. I start the engine, he unties the lines, and I back her out of the slip. As if we had been doing it forever, we are off, cruising down the Town River toward the open harbor. I have anticipated the actual instant of being underway in the boat I worked and obsessed over for a long time. Somehow I miss the moment now. I am too busy or preoccupied or somehow disconnected, but once we travel down the first short stretches of river and make the turn out into the open water, I feel great. Better than great, I am soaring. The motor is on and the mainsail is up, pulling just a bit. The bow splashes through the salt water. I feel the first gentle breezes from the sea on my face. It all hits me. The pride in this accomplishment, the joy of being on the water, the sudden realization that I now actually have my own boat after all those years of standing on docks and looking and yearning. I become ecstatically happy.

It should have gone on like this for the rest of the day. Rich and

I should have gone out through Hull Gut and on to Boston Light at least, as we have on so many other days, in so many other sailboats, but things don't go as we might expect, or even as we think we deserve. Before I have unfurled the jib, the engine quits. It refuses to restart. We are adrift in the ferry channel to Boston. The afternoon feels different. A little chillier. I get the jib out before we drift into shallow water. We soon have her sailing and under control. As we turn and sail back the way we have just come, the breeze freshens to blow in our faces. We end this first trip in my new boat with an awkward, spread-eagled landing under sail at the marina slip. Rich keeps her from smashing the dock.

I spend the next three days on my knees in the cabin with my head in the engine compartment, learning the art of bleeding a diesel engine. The consensus is that after all the work I had done on her fuel system, there is still air in there, somewhere, or maybe I have a bad fuel pump. In his book *This Old Boat*, Don Casey says something to the effect that the problem with gasoline engines is keeping the fuel in and the problem with diesel engines is keeping the air out. One of my neighbors at the marina, Nick, the owner of a nicely rebuilt 28-foot Ericson, who has generously helped me with a few other problems, is now telling me about the virtues of gasoline power. As he talks the large pirate flag tied to his boat's rigging flaps behind him in the breeze. I hear from others on the dock that the Coast Guard boarded his boat a few days earlier to stop him from flying the Jolly Roger while underway.

One slip further over a recently launched wooden cabin cruiser has an emergency pump in her bilge wired to shore power. Every thirty minutes she shoots a stream of water out of her bilge with the force of a jet engine, enough water to fill several bathtubs. As the pump runs you can see her lift several inches on her lines. The pump goes off. She begins to settle. In half an hour the pump will fire up again. It is spring in the marina. We all have our problems.

We have our problems, but I have never met a friendlier bunch of guys than at this marina. Everyone seems ready to lend a hand or a tool. Pete, who lives in Quincy, tells me it is the brotherhood of the

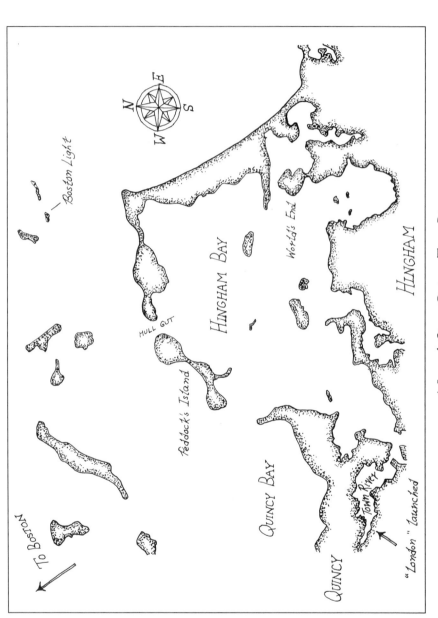

LONDON's Launch Site—Quincy Town River

sea and the boatyard. I think it is also the neighborhood. I like Quincy.

After bleeding the fuel system, I let the engine run. It will run for fifteen to maybe thirty minutes and then just quit. It will not restart until I bleed it again. I go through the process over and over, trying something a little different each time. Early one Saturday morning, on my way to the marina, I stop at a marine store and pick up Nigel Calder's book *Boatowner's Mechanical and Electrical Manual* to see what he has to say on the subject of bleeding. As I read I come to realize I have not been bleeding the complete fuel system. I race back to the boat and try a new method. By early afternoon, the engine has run for an hour before I shut her off. That's done! I feel another surge of pride at solving a difficult problem and fixing it myself. The next day I enjoy a successful Sunday sail with my wife Nancy, my friend Bruce, and his young son John, who amuses us by using his dad's binoculars to read the chart while we sail among Boston's harbor islands.

It is time to move LONDON to her summer mooring on Buzzards Bay. The night before Pete and I are due to depart, the manual bilge pump comes apart in my hands as I am trying to pump the boat dry. I call Pete and postpone our departure one more day. I do not want to set off until I have everything working. I have sailed often enough to know how quickly things break and go wrong underway. I want at least to begin the voyage with a completely working boat.

The next day I am able to rebuild this, the last pump on the boat—the only pump I haven't yet overhauled—with parts I have on hand. The following morning Pete and I pull away from the marina as Sandy takes pictures. We plan to sail out of Boston Harbor and turn south to cruise just off the coast, past the old Massachusetts coastal towns of Cohasset, Scituate, and Plymouth toward the entrance of the Cape Cod Canal. Once through the canal, we will sail down Buzzards Bay, almost to New Bedford. It is a distance of about 80 nautical miles. We plan to take our time and enjoy the trip, spending two nights sleeping on the boat. Sailboats are required to motor through the canal, and to make good time we need to hit the

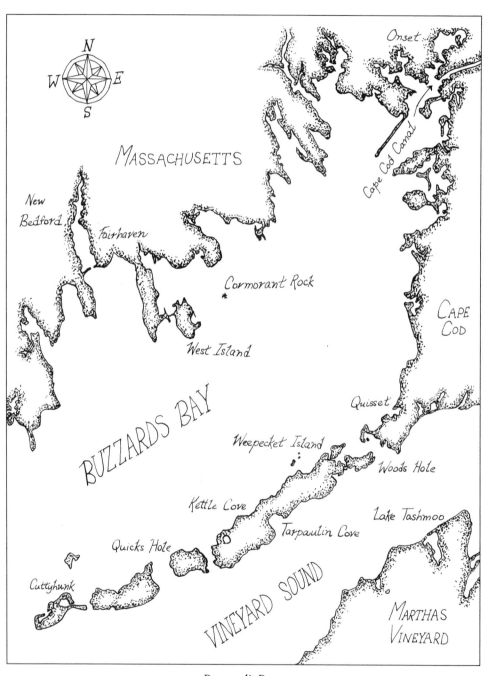

Buzzard's Bay

tides right, as the canal current averages around 4 knots. We leave early to catch the evening ebb tide at the canal entrance.

We have a good breeze, averaging perhaps 20 knots all day out of the west. It is a changeable day, with rainsqualls off Plymouth's beaches in the afternoon. LONDON really shows her stuff, sailing at times better than 6 knots according to the knot meter. This surprises me. I thought her full-keeled hull would provide a comfortable but somewhat stately ride; instead we can often coax her into a brisk run.

The wind is with us until we round the Mary Ann Rocks off Manomet Point. We power the last 8 miles to the canal so that we will make the tide and have daylight through its length. Not far from the canal entrance mark, the engine quits and will not restart. While we drift I bleed the engine and then it starts. Sailing is not permitted in the canal; power is required. We motor into the canal with Pete at the helm and me stationed near the engine with my wrenches laid out on the bunk, ready to bleed her again at a moment's notice. We are lucky. The engine gets us through, but I no longer trust it.

This is how it will go over the next few weeks. Most of the time the diesel engine, which I am now calling "Old Reliable" in the hope that this incantation will somehow induce a consistent performance, will rumble on, but at those moments when the most is at stake, she will, with a cussedness that almost drives me overboard, cough, sputter, and then stop with a rattle and a shake. I begin to associate that last mechanical shudder with a sinking feeling in my stomach.

On my first solo sail in LONDON, at the entrance to Woods Hole Passage, I am standing at the mast lowering the main for the passage through the current, and just as I think, "This would be a terrible place for the engine to quit," I notice it has gotten very quiet. Watching our slow drift toward the rocks to lee, I sigh with resignation, quickly raise the mainsail, tack my way into a cove, drop the anchor, step into the cabin, and kneel down before "Old Reliable" and bleed her again. A diesel makes a kind of sighing sound as you bleed the air out of the fuel lines. I feel she is sighing for me.

On a day when the small craft warnings are up, Bruce and I are making our way through the dogleg in the channel leading back to my mooring. Exactly where the channel is the narrowest, with submerged ledges to either side, she quits again. Bruce makes what is now becoming the familiar rush to the bow and tosses the anchor over. I go below to bleed "Old Reliable."

"You have got to get this fixed." Bruce seems annoyed.

On a day Nancy and I spend sitting on the boat waiting for the wind to drop as LONDON swings back and forth on her mooring pendant, we try something new with some duct tape and a bicycle pump. I disconnect the vent hose from the fuel tank and seal the opening with duct tape. I then attach a needle valve on the end of the bicycle pump hose and use it to pierce the duct tape covering the vent. While Nancy *gently* uses the pump to pressurize the tank, I assume my position in front of the engine. As the air pressure forces the fuel into the system, I blot around the fuel lines and fuel filters with clean, dry paper towels, looking for leaks, spots on the paper towel. If it leaks fuel when being pressurized like this, it will leak air when the fuel pump is sucking under load. We find fuel is oozing out around the fitting to the new fuel filter. The fittings and clamps are as tight as they can be, but the fuel is leaking out through the metal threads of the fittings. I remove all the threaded fittings from the filter, spread a liquid rubber gasket on their threads, and screw them back in nice and snug. I bleed the engine again.

"Old Reliable" will now run through the summer and fall without any further trouble. As the summer progresses, the problems with the mechanics of the boat fade away. I can now focus on cruises along the southern New England coast, what to eat, who to have aboard, and where to anchor for the remainder of LONDON's first season afloat. I can even begin to think about the other changes I need to make to her.

Complete List of Work Done to LONDON (née LOON) from October 1998 to October 1999

OVERALL
Sand all exterior teak to bare wood and apply two coats of Cetol.
Remove everything from boat and scrub inside and out—three times.
Add hawsepipe to foredeck.
Perform cosmetic fiberglass repair at keel foot.
Replace all extruded bungs in toerail with teak plugs.

MAST
Replace all three halyards with New England Ropes ³⁄₈-inch Sta-Set X
   polyester braid.
Replace masthead/steaming light.
Add anchor light at mast top.
Replace VHF antenna.
Scrub mast.

FRESHWATER SYSTEM
Remove water tank, clean, and reinstall.
Add deck water fill and pipe into water tank.
Replace all freshwater hoses with series 168 reinforced clear tubing.
Add new 1-micron Aqua City water filter.
Replace water faucet with a new Fynspray Galley Spout.
Replace water pump with a foot pump (Whale Gusher MKIII).
Replace sink drain hose.
Remove sink drain through-hull and seacock, rebuild, and reinstall.

HEAD SYSTEM
Remove existing sewage holding tank and destroy.
Remove all existing hoses and replace with new hose.
Buy and install new holding tank.
Remove, rebuild, and reinstall manual pump (Whale Gusher 10).
Remove 1¹⁄₂-inch outtake through-hull and seacock. Replace seacock
   and reinstall.
Remove ³⁄₄-inch intake through-hull and seacock, rebuild, and reinstall.

Install new 1½-inch bronze vented loop.
Install new Whale Y-valve.
Purchase Headmate spares kit for head.

ENGINE COOLING
Remove intake through-hull and seacock, rebuild, and reinstall.
Install new Groco seawater filter.
Replace all cooling hoses.

ENGINE FUEL SYSTEMS
Remove existing fuel tank and replace with new 12-gallon metal tank.
Install new Racor 120 diesel filter with water trap.
Replace all flexible fuel lines.

ENGINE
Purchase complete parts kit for boat.

GALLEY
Replace existing pressurized alcohol stove with new non-pressurized
  Origo 4000 alcohol stove.

BILGE PUMPS
Rebuild manual bilge pump (Whale Gusher).
Add new Rule automatic electric bilge pump.

ELECTRICAL SYSTEM AND LIGHTS
Install two new batteries.
Clean and test all connections.
Install new grounding plate.
Install two new halogen berth lights in main cabin.
Rewire and restore navigation lights.
Rewire spotlight.
Replace cigarette lighter light and socket with new one.
Replace antenna coaxial lines and connectors for VHF radio.

INSTRUMENTS AND NAVIGATION
Install new Raytheon Autohelm ST+ 2000 auto-tiller.
Install new barometer in main cabin.
Remove and service knot meter impeller.

SAILS
Have leech line of little jib repaired.

5

Anchoring LONDON

Once "Old Reliable" actually becomes reliable, I take more friends out for day trips. We sail through warm breezes, and when needed the engine responds. Buzzards Bay has plenty of wind. As I spend more time on the bay, the daily patterns of the winds become familiar. As I sail LONDON week after week and begin to understand her capabilities, a few problems emerge. I will fix them over the winter. One problem I need to fix now.

Although I acquired a tiller steering system with LONDON, it has refused to function. I can use it as a stick to hold the tiller in place, but it is otherwise useless. I need the auto-tiller to free me to do other things when I am either sailing alone or sailing with passengers who are better left without duties.

I ask one of my friends who has an electrical engineering degree to look the unit over. He can't get it working. He recommends I replace it, all the additional encouragement I need to buy a new tiller steering system. It's expensive, but I know from the moment I open the box and revel in its solid simplicity that it is well designed.

Since the boat is already in the water, I will do the installation on the mooring. Early one morning in June while the water is calm and the wind still, I row out to LONDON with all the equipment I need: epoxy resin and hardener, disposable gloves, a pre-cut plywood backing plate, a fully-charged portable drill, and a carpenter's square. Screwdrivers and wire cutting and crimping tools are already on the boat.

The project will involve installing a metal socket for the foot of the tiller's mechanical arm in the cockpit seat and epoxying it and the backing plate in place; mounting a six-prong socket in the cockpit wall and wiring that to the battery; and finally installing a protruding steel pin into the top of the arm of my beautiful teak tiller. The pin and the socket need to be positioned exactly. I measure three times before I am sure I have my marks properly located, drill the holes, and mix the epoxy. I do the wiring while the epoxy hardens, eat lunch, and by early afternoon I am running *auto* through calibration and "sea trials" in Nasketucket Bay.

I can put the boat on a course, set the sails, and turn the steering over to *auto*. The boat will follow whatever compass course I have set. I am free to move about the boat, to do other things. With all this freedom comes a new danger: If I fall off the boat while LONDON and *auto* are running things they will blithely sail away. I resolve to stay in the boat and not give them the chance.

In midsummer my friend Pete plans to come sailing with me again for a few days. It will be our first overnight cruise since bringing LONDON to Buzzards Bay. We are going to Nantucket.

We cross Buzzards Bay from Fairhaven in good time and with a steady wind blowing out of the south are able to sail through Woods Hole Passage without resorting to the engine. Later in the afternoon we make our way across to the Vineyard and steam up the little channel into Martha's Vineyard's Lake Tashmoo. It is July 16, 1999.

That evening I can just see LONDON from my vantage point on the little beach at Lake Tashmoo. She is anchored way out past the moored boats in mid-pond. I help Pete drag the dinghy out of the water and turn it over, and we scramble up the bank to walk the back roads into Vineyard Haven. Cars just off the ferry arrive at gray-shingled vacation homes in the sandy woods. Screen doors bang open. Wind chimes ring out Zen-like mantras across the yards of thin dry grass, sand, and dead pine needles. There is laughter and the gentle tinkle of ice in cold glasses. The air is warm and fragrant with the scent of pine and the promise of a beautiful weekend.

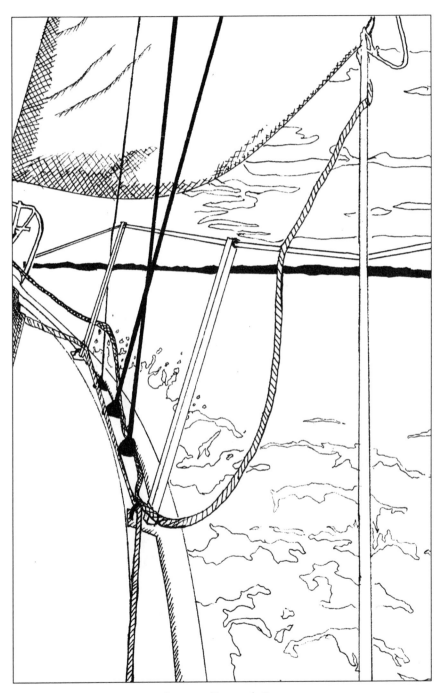

Crossing Buzzards Bay

It is a twenty-five-minute walk into town. We decide to eat at the
inn. Pete and I talk about our plans for the four days we have free.
We eat grilled striped bass fresh off a local boat and drink some
wine. After dinner we walk down to look at the harbor and then
begin to wander back to the boat, leaving the noise and lights of
Vineyard Haven behind. In the dusky light, cabin windows cast a
golden glow into the piney woods. The air is breezy and a little
damp. I have sand in my sandals. It is the height of summer in
Massachusetts.

We push the dinghy off the beach for the short row out to the
boat in the dark. Pete is a great guy to have along on a cruise. He
loves to row, has sailed these waters for years, and is great company.
While Pete rows he tells me how years ago he and his brother had
just finished their plywood sailboat in time to set off on a night sail
from Quincy to Marblehead for a race the following morning. I
lounge in the stern watching the boats and the stars drift by, until I
realize LONDON is not there. She is not where we left her, nowhere
in sight. I tell him the boat is gone. He spins around to look for himself and then digs the oars in to get us closer to where we had left
her anchored, next to another sailboat, a Bayfield from Mystic,
Connecticut.

Dark little wavelets splash against the hard dinghy. It is very quiet.
For a moment we just drift and look. I try to think what could have
happened. Overhead a fresh breeze pushes strands of hazy cloud
through the tall treetops that line the shores of Lake Tashmoo. On
the surface is barely a ripple. We don't say anything for a few
minutes. We are all adrift.

I hear movement in the dark cockpit of the Bayfield and then a
voice.

"I bet you two are wondering where your boat is."

"Have you seen her?"

"Oh, I've seen her all right. I saw her get up and go when the tide
changed."

My heart sank. To have this happen after all that work.

"Don't worry. I tied her to a mooring off there near that light."

He points over to the far shore where a light stands atop a private dock. I can't make out LONDON in the gloom. He had been sitting on deck when he saw LONDON move away, dragging her anchor and drifting down toward the moored boats near the beach.

"There was a powerboat going by and I hailed him. We chased your boat down. When we got close he pulled alongside so I could step over onto her. I pulled the anchor up and then took a line from the fisherman. We towed your boat over to a mooring he knew would be free. It's across the Pond. Over there near that dock light."

He apologized for getting mud on the deck.

"There's grass here. You need something more than that little Danforth you got on there."

I remember now when we had been swimming earlier. I'd watched the big Canada geese dive and then surface to pull the grass stems through their shelly beaks. How could I thank him enough?

"It was nothing."

We try to make him understand how grateful and humbled we are by his kindness. Maybe we overdid it. I think we just embarrassed him and ended up rowing away in silence when he vanished below.

Pete rowed us toward the dock light. As we slip through the dark I remember how maybe a dozen summers before I had been at an ocean beach on a day when the waves were high and curling in with a boom, followed by the sound of sand and gravel being washed back out to sea. I was playing in the surf, way out on a sandbar with my tough little six-year-old daughter, who at this age could never get enough of the sea. We both heard the cries for help. A man dragged himself past us. He seemed exhausted as he slogged toward shore. He looked over at us.

"That's it for me. I can't reach him."

I looked out to sea and saw a boy lift in the wave curl.

"Help!" he cried.

Another wave blocked him from my view. I told Kate to go for help on shore. Once she was on her way I began to work my way further out into the surf.

Before I reached for the boy I lost my footing. Sand swirled beneath my feet and I too was swept away by the surge. I grabbed the boy, swallowed some water, and for a moment thought I had made a mistake. Now there were two of us out here in the rip. But with him still in hand, I found that if I arched my back as the waves broke over us, the waves themselves would drive us forward toward shore and onto the sandbar. With two more waves we were safely back on the sandbar, standing waist deep in the rushing water, looking around and breathing deeply. I looked over at the boy. He stuck out his tongue. I let go of his hand.

Suddenly a lifeguard was next to us trailing a line that ran back to a giant spool on the beach. Another guard splashed by on his way to someone else caught further out. Everyone else was out of the water, watching us.

Later, as I sat on the beach in the warm sun, the man who had staggered past me earlier came over with the boy I'd grabbed. It was his son. They came to thank me. I was embarrassed by the thanks in the same way we must have embarrassed Captain Bayfield.

We found LONDON in the dark part of the pond, much closer to the trees on shore. Once aboard we didn't say much to each other that night.

I knew I had made a serious mistake in anchoring—wrong anchor, not properly set, I should have known better. I guess Pete knew it too but saw no need to point it out to me. Without Captain Bayfield's help, who knows where this boat I had worked so hard to refloat would be now. Up on the beach I guess, having banged a few other boats on the way in.

I got into my bunk and settled down to read more of Arthur Ransome's *We Didn't Mean to Go to Sea* for the second time. In this book a group of kids are left alone on a sailboat while their skipper makes a quick trip ashore for some fuel and *when the tide changes* they are swept out of the harbor and into the English Channel. The oldest boy takes on the role of captain and manages to sail downwind to Holland. It is a wonderful book. I'd first read it when I was about the same age as that boy on the beach, about eleven. I think I will take the name of their dinghy, IMP, and paint it on my own. The sailboat in the story was named GOBLIN. GOBLIN and IMP.

Ransome led an interesting life. His first marriage was a disaster. Unable to secure a divorce, he moved to Russia, where he was a correspondent for a British newspaper. He played chess with Lenin and beat him, was acquainted with Trotsky, and reported on the Russian Revolution. He spent much of his life messing around in sailboats—in England's Lake District, on the English Channel, and while in Russia on the Baltic. His sailing experiences enlivened the series of children's books he is best known for, *Swallows and Amazons*.

Captain Bayfield has reminded me, as Pete often says, that out on the water people will go out of their way, *way* out of their way, to help one another. I vowed then and there that if I ever had the chance to help someone else, I would. In this way we could atone for the trouble we had caused.

The next morning we start early to clear the entrance of Tashmoo while the tide is slack, but perhaps also so we can slip away while everyone else is still in bed. The Bayfield is quiet, still asleep, as we pass. We pick our way through the narrow channels, the shallow rips, and finally pop out of Tashmoo into a roaring morning on Vineyard Sound. The first thing I notice is one and then another Coast Guard boat racing by. The small craft warnings are up. The wind will be behind us all day. Late in the morning when I talk to my wife on the cell phone we learn that John Kennedy, Jr's plane crashed off the Vineyard the previous night. It must have happened about the same time we were drifting around in Tashmoo looking for LONDON.

After heading north on Vineyard Sound, we round the two Chops and turn toward Nantucket. We poke through a midday dead spot off Cape Poge, but the afternoon develops into the proverbial sleigh ride. We have all the sails up full, just backing the main a bit to avoid being overpowered in the gusts. I have snapshots from that afternoon. Pete pulls at the tiller as the boat heels over. He is braced against the opposite side of the cockpit. Behind him you can see our wake splash against the windblown white caps.

We arrive in Nantucket Harbor a little after 3:30 in the afternoon and immediately start calling on the VHF for a mooring. They tell us to try again at 4:40. We cruise through the inner harbor. It seems that no one is planning to leave. The wind is whipping across the surface of the water, and people are huddled behind their dodgers. Boats cling to the moorings.

We find a spot way out in the northeast section of Nantucket Harbor and set our anchor down near a big old yawl. On our first attempt the anchor does not set; on our second attempt we seem to get a solid grip on the bottom. After we have been there for a bit, it is clear there aren't going to be any free moorings today, for us or for the man we heard earlier pleading for a mooring on the VHF, yelling into his microphone, "I don't have the ground tackle for these conditions!" No one seems to be leaving the harbor. The wind howls.

Pete gets in the dinghy and rows up to the bow, and I pass the second, bigger Danforth to him under the rail. As I pay the line out he rows like mad against the wind to a spot where he can drop it well off to one side of the first anchor. After we are sure we are secure, we call for the launch. The Nantucket Harbor launches are big and they are fast. They will come all the way out to where we have anchored and give the other passengers a nice tour of this remote corner of the harbor. Only one driver over the course of our three-day visit would ask if we could have anchored any further away. We give him a few extra bucks. He gives us a fast ride into town and a hint about where we might find a hot shower.

On the first night, after a dinner in town and just after lights out, I am settled in the forward V-berth. There is a tremendous crash inches from my head. I shoot out of my bunk yelling like a fool.

"We've been hit! We've been hit!"

Pete and I hurry up on deck to see a big powerboat swirling by downwind. A man and then a woman come up on deck from below. Like us they are only half-dressed. As he drifts away the man yells over to us, "You ran into us!"

We look again at our anchor lines and over at the yawl next to us and then yell back.

"No! You are adrift. You hit us! We are at anchor."

He would apologize later. There is no damage to the Cape Dory.

The next afternoon, during nap time, I again feel something is wrong. At first I dismiss it. I tell myself that after the collision and LONDON's disappearance the other night, I am just getting jumpy. But the feeling persists. I sit up and look out my porthole to see the big yawl, which had been our reference point, our stable mark, slide out of view astern. She is dragging her anchor and drifting toward the sandbars downwind. No one is on deck. We try to call her on the VHF and then try the harbormaster. We have no luck reaching either, but eventually do get the Coast Guard at Brant Point. A few minutes later the yawl's master appears on deck. He again anchors her adjacent to us.

Late that night we are awakened to horns blaring, shouting, and big diesel engines revving. Off to the north a whole series of boats are moving and resetting their anchors. Spotlights wiggle in the gloom, licking the tips of the turbulent waves with their beams. Chains rattle in the dark. Only bad dreams tonight.

Until this trip, I'd never worried much about anchoring—I'd never had any trouble. This trip would forever cure me of that innocent indifference. I begin to think about what additional ground tackle LONDON should carry.

6

Winter 1999–2000

At the end of the season I decide to sail LONDON from Buzzards Bay up the Massachusetts coast to Boston Light and then into Quincy's Town River, where she was launched. This is where she will be hauled out. It will be a kind of homecoming after the first season.

My friend Bruce comes along on the trip north. We leave Fairhaven early in the morning and are near the entrance to Boston Harbor at twilight. We are sailing well. The running lights are on. The sea is flat enough for me to make us a hot dinner in the galley. We eat on deck and watch flock after flock of birds coming in from the ocean. They swoop out of the now dark east, becoming recognizable as bird forms only as they pass across the patch of lighter sky overhead. They flutter and squawk, rush past the zenith, and flee into the last of the late evening's western purple glow, bound for their night roosts. It is primeval. I think there must be a million birds out here, birds that move only under the cover of dusk and in great numbers. They keep coming in flock after flock. They seem to be headed for the marshes around World's End.

LONDON will dock at Town River about a week before she is hauled out. During that time I get in a few final day sails. One cold blustery day I take my parents out. The sky is gray. The genoa sheet keeps slipping off the cleat. We go out through Hull Gut into Nantasket Roads, admire Boston Light out on Little Brewster, and come back through West Gut. The harbor islands are a world unto themselves. Situated across Boston Harbor's 50 square miles of water, the islands are quiet places forgotten by most of the twenty-five million people who surround them.

At the Maritime Museum in Greenwich, England I have seen the charts of the harbor drawn by Joseph F.W. Des Barres that the British had in 1775 at the beginning of the American Revolution. Most of the islands appear in some recognizable shape, although many of the names are different. Peddock's Island was Puttock on the old chart; Little Brewster was known as Light House Island. I wonder about the word *puttock* and look it up. There are two possible derivations: first an Old English word meaning a tract of wet marshy land, and second an alternative form of *futtock*, the curved rib timber in an old ship, somewhat resembling the shape of the island itself.

Boston Harbor is noticeably cleaner than when I first began to sail here. The new sewage treatment plants have made the difference. Before we were boatowners, Rich and I sailed for several years at the Boston Harbor Sailing Club. In 1991, when we were taking lessons in the handling of cruising boats at the club, there were still spots out here where on the outgoing tide there was an upwelling of raw polluted water. That is gone now. We see an improvement in water quality, sea life, and odor, even under the piers of downtown Boston.

When Des Barres was here it must have been a natural paradise. It was also different geographically. Boston is the most physically changed of the American cities. These changes have included areas of the islands. There has been filling and leveling, which continues even today, as the debris from all the highway and tunnel construction in Boston is moved by barge to reshape Spectacle Island. The Boston Harbor Islands National Recreation Area was established in 1996 to protect thirty-four islands totaling some 1,600 acres of land in a national park that stretches seaward 11 miles from downtown Boston.

———— ❦ ————

LONDON's first summer season has been a success. I have taken eight groups of friends sailing and have not lost or injured a soul. The boat has not sunk. We have not run aground. We have not been boarded. However, in Lake Tashmoo LONDON went adrift, and in Nantucket we suffered a collision.

Having sailed through the season I now know what changes need to be made, and I have a long list of boat improvements for the winter. The stuffing box continues to leak; the bilge is constantly wet. The sump pump can keep up with the leak, but I worry what would happen if I had to leave the boat for a month. Would the batteries run out of juice?

The roller-furler that came with the boat is an old-style furler. The big genoa has a wire luff, which the sail wraps around when furled. The tack of the sail is attached to a rotating drum, which spools the furling line. The sail can only be furled when it is luffing, not under any tension[4]. If the wind is strong it is a chore to roll in my genoa, especially for the first few turns. A few times the sail has wrapped around the wire and created flaps of cloth that continue to flog until the wrap is rolled out and redone. I need a modern roller-furler with an extrusion running up the headstay and bearings in the roller, so that leverage is applied along the entire length of the sail's luff for a smoother wrapping operation.

LONDON is hauled at Town River at the end of October and again trucked to her spot next to our garage at home. I winterize her, unload her, and then leave her alone.

The snow begins to fall. A few days after Christmas, Nancy and I drive down to Wickford, Rhode Island. We wander around the town and eat out, but the big excitement for me is picking through all the old pieces of boat that line the shelves of a local marine consignment store. From among the selection of old hatches and Lorans, I select a used 25-pound CQR anchor, a fuel gauge, and a flag pole.

The next day work begins again on the boat. When I did the engine work during the initial restoration, I bypassed a large, old fuel filter, but left it in place. I now dig down into that part of the engine compartment and pull it out. It goes to the dump. The diesel fuel goes into the recycled oil drum, the metal parts go on the scrap pile.

The flush pump for the head has been leaking. This is not as bad as it sounds, as it is clean sea water that squirts out when the pump is operated. I remove the head flush pump from the boat and take it apart in my workshop. I replace all the little springs, gaskets, and diaphragms using a parts kit I have. Then I reinstall the pump on the side of the head in the boat. These two jobs take an entire day.

From some scrap pieces of redwood I make a three-pocket cubby shelf and install it under the companionway steps. Here I will keep tubes of sunscreen, dish soap, et al.

The next big project is the traveler. LONDON came with a traditional triangular block arrangement for the mainsheet. There are two blocks mounted behind the aft corners of the cockpit. The sheet ran from a single block with a becket in one corner, through a double block hung on the boom bail, down to the other fixed single block, back up to the boom, and finally to a mid-cockpit cleat. I can't get the boom amidships on a beat with this arrangement. I plan to install a traveler track across the rear of the cockpit and rig the mainsheet to a car riding along it.

I pore over hardware catalogs for weeks. I place my order on January 2 and the parts come a few days later. I have chosen an anodized black track. There are blocks and cams at each end of the traveler track and a car riding along the track on bearings with blocks atop it. The mainsheet fiddle block will be attached to the car. This means I will have a movable mainsheet attachment point and should be able to get the boom in the middle of the boat when I am heading upwind. This should improve LONDON's ability to sail, especially into the wind.

I need to fashion a wood base on which to mount the new traveler. I pick through my supply of wood until I find a piece of mahogany. Then I remove the old blocks and the cleat from LONDON's rear deck at the back of the cockpit. I need to shape the wood to fit both the gently curving rear edge of the cockpit and the camber of the deck. I cut, trim, and taper, climb up to the boat, try the fit, and go back to the shop to adjust. Once I have the shaping done, I soak the piece and clamp it over wood blocks so that it takes on its new bent form.

In mid-January I send in the first article about LONDON's rebuild to *Good Old Boat* magazine. It is accepted a week later. I am elated but it will be a year before I see it in print.

I buy a kit for an anchor sail and complete sewing it in early February. I install simple fuel and electric charge gauges in the boat on a new wood instrument panel I have made. I order a handheld VHF radio.

LONDON's lifelines are in sad shape. I take them off the boat and up to a marine store in Peabody that does rigging work and has a selection of used parts. They remake my lifelines and also assemble the roller-furler I have selected.

I order luff tape for the genoa to match the new roller-furler. I need to remove the old wire line from the sail's luff, clean up that edge, and then sew the luff tape in place. I am able to do this sewing with our home machine until I get to the head of the sail, where the multiple layers of sail cloth are just too thick. I toss the genoa in a wheelbarrow and push it down the street to pay my friend Steve a visit. He has a powerful sewing machine. With his help I soon have it finished.

From the marine store I finally get the machine screws that fit in the stanchion bases and hold the stanchions in place. If you pulled up on a lifeline during the first sailing season, the stanchions would lift up out of their bases. Some passengers found this disquieting. I don't know why. I would always put them back.

At the beginning of March I install the wood base and then the traveler track on the boat. I fasten the traveler track using many stainless bolts with large stainless fender washers and plywood strips serving as backing plates. I rig the control lines. This is one project that comes out particularly well. The wood matches the cockpit coaming in color and grain well enough to look like original work. The mechanism is well placed and it works. I can get the boom where I want it. LONDON's sail trim is greatly improved.

I now remove the engine's raw water intake screen plate and clean and paint it. I clean, inspect, and lubricate all the old turnbuckles. The turnbuckles are the closed stainless kind, basically tapered, forged steel tubes with internal threads. I discover the insides of these are packed with dirt and grime. This is something else I did not get to in the first winter of work. It takes several days to get all these threads and turnbuckles cleaned. Although they are filthy, they all seem sound.

To begin work on the new dodger I am going to build, I use the lines running overhead to hoist the mast off the boat and leave it suspended above. I now have enough blocks so this is a one-man job. With the deck clear I begin to fabricate the template for the dodger. First I get the tubing cut and bent. I assemble it in place, holding it temporarily in position with long strips of masking tape. Then I fit a pattern sheet over the frame, tape it in place, and adjust and mark it. This process starts well enough, but a breeze comes up later in the afternoon and causes slight errors in my measurements. I am too stubborn to quit. As the pattern starts to blow around another pair of hands would have been useful, but my family is off somewhere. Once I have my pattern templates made for the dodger cloth, I remove them and the metal frame. Then I lower the mast back onto the boat.

Over the course of this working season I will try several times to tighten the packing gland nut and lessen the drip from the stuffing box. It is such an awkward position that I never succeed.

On one nice weekend in early April I replace the anchor light bulb, organize the 12-volt spares, charge the batteries and put them back in the boat, Cetol all the teak, clean up the mast wire connections, paint the boot stripe red, and caulk around the cockpit.

We discovered that water streaming down the deck on a rough day will seep through the cockpit coamings and run across the seats. This proved to be unpleasant. Nobody likes a wet seat.

The small round hawsepipe I had initially installed on the foredeck, while large enough for the chain and the rope, turned out not to pass the shackle used to join them. I now remove this pipe and replace it with a much larger deck pipe.

In the final four weeks before the May 11, 2000 launch target, I install new stern cleats in the hard dinghy, pick up the new roller-furler with its new headstay, finish sewing the dodger and fit it with new snaps onto the cabintop, apply more Cetol to the teak in the cockpit and along the toerails, run the engine, restore the water system and fill the tank, check all the hose clamps and seacocks, paint the bottom, paint the inside of one locker, and install a new GPS next to the depth meter on the aft bulkhead of the cabin. I planned to install the GPS's antenna on the stern rail, but I find that I get a decent signal with the antenna left inside the electrical compartment. There it will stay.

The docks are not yet in at Town River, so after LONDON slips off the submerged boat trailer I tie her up to a fishing float midstream in the river. I spend the rest of the afternoon bending on the sails, running the lines, and getting her shipshape. I eat and sleep aboard and then at 5:30 the next morning untie from the float and head downriver.

It is a nice morning, cool and sunny with some high clouds to the southwest. By 7:00 A.M. I have passed Boston Light and am heading toward Cohasset. I take the inside passage among the rocks along The Gangway and past the West Willies to exit outside of South Entering Rock. I will be off Scituate by 9:00. While the auto-tiller steers the boat, I wash and scrub her down. I am nearly at the Cape Cod Canal by 2:30 P.M., and while waiting for the current to be in my favor I sail back and forth, tacking into the southwest. On one of these tacks an inner shroud pops loose. I refasten it and half an hour later, the one on the other side unscrews. I drop the sails and drift while I go over all the standing rigging carefully. The tide will begin to ebb at 6:09 P.M. I make my entrance to the canal from Cape Cod Bay at 5:20 and am past the Onset channel on the Buzzards Bay end by 7:00. Rich has driven from Concord to pick me up. It is dark when I row up to the dinghy dock at my marina. I can hear his steps on the floating dock.

"Hi Rich."

"Hello Captain."

"What a long day. Cold too. On the other side of the canal, I was wearing all the clothes I had."

"Okay, let's get in the car. The heat's on."

Even so cold and tired, even so grumpy, I am happy to have LONDON back on her mooring. The season has begun. Late in the summer this year I will be heading to Maine for the first extended cruise in my own boat.

7

LONDON's Lines

Since I keep my sailboat moored in Fairhaven, Massachusetts I am often reminded of Joshua Slocum. He rebuilt SPRAY here before setting sail in the early 1890s for his historic single-handed circumnavigation. On the other side of the neck there is a monument to him near the field where he did his restoration. He had been given SPRAY by a New Bedford whaling captain, Eben Pierce, who said to him, "Come to Fairhaven and I will give you a ship[5]." It would be a ship in need of extensive work. There are still plenty of old and restored boats in Fairhaven's harbors and boatyards to help LONDON feel at home.

Although I am not embarking on a solo world cruise, but on a summer coastal cruise to Maine, I would like to think that while Joshua might have smiled at my excitement over such a small voyage, he would certainly have appreciated my sailboat. The Cape Dorys are built in the traditional style, full-keeled and sturdy. They are not particularly fast boats, but sea-friendly and strong. Just as Joshua sought out tough white "pasture" oak for the structure, Cape Dory built their exceptionally strong hulls with abundant and carefully laid fiberglass. They too were locally made.

From my mooring I can look across Nasketucket Bay toward the green fields and houses of Mattapoisett. I wonder what this would have looked like in Slocum's time. I imagine there would have been fewer houses and farms and less stuff in the water. Today the moorings, the buoys, the lobster pots, and hundreds of blue plastic floats belonging to the aquaculture farm are floating around out there.

I turn on the instruments and get ready to cast off. The depth at the mooring reads 7 feet. The mooring pendant hits the water with a splash. Her bow falls slowly off in the regular midday southwest breeze and LONDON is soon running easily through the small harbor waves. As I head out the channel and into the bay, the earth's solid surface sinks further and further below us. I picture this as a two-dimensional cut-away graphic in motion on some video device, drawn in unreal primary colors. My little boat bobs above the gently descending line tracing the landscape of the sea floor. A few fish pass beneath unawares. The water depth increases. We gather speed. The seriously deep water of Maine lies days ahead.

There is a good breeze across Nasketucket Bay, and for a time the water deepens to more than 20 feet. Under full sail I slip through an unmarked passage, 12 feet deep, between the rows of the aquaculture buoys and Ram Island, enter Buzzards Bay itself, and cross the entrance channel to Mattapoisett Harbor. I turn toward the Cape Cod Canal, where in less than two hours the tide will begin to turn in my favor. The water at this end of the bay is about 30 feet deep, and that will hold through the canal. These are generally shallow waters with a sand-mud bottom between the rocky areas. The depths change gradually, nothing like the sudden changes in depth I will soon see in Maine.

With the boat sailing under the control of the auto-tiller, I run through my mental checklist, one last time. The simple things come first—food, water, fuel—then I check the bilge, battery levels, spare fuel tank, extra oil, scan the lines for wear and take a turn around the deck looking at the turnbuckles and up the mast.

About 9:00 that night LONDON and I slip into Scituate Harbor, 19 nautical miles south of Boston. It is dark. I call the harbor launch on the VHF and am led through the dark quiet anchorage to a vacant mooring. It is a warm evening with little wind. Several small sailboats glide among the moored boats in the dark. Their crews whisper as they pass. One large white sail moves by—dimly, faintly, as if possessed. A creak of a rudder and the sail begins to flap and then falls with a whoosh. The main halyard sings through the air. I hear knocking in a dinghy, the splash of oars, and then all is quiet. I climb into my bunk with a volume of Joseph Conrad and am soon absorbed in the story of the ship NARCISSUS on her homeward run.

> Under white wings she skimmed low over the blue sea like a great tired bird speeding to its nest. The clouds raced with her mastheads; they rose astern enormous and white, soared to the zenith, flew past, and falling down the wide curve of the sky, seemed to dash headlong into the sea—the clouds swifter than the ship, more free, but without a home.

In the morning I go to the harbormaster's hut and shower. The harbormaster and I talk for half an hour, of this and that, of the diesel engine that ran for a year, storms in this harbor, and what may come. Scituate is one of my favorite harbors. It has great facilities for the transient and the people are friendly. There are not many New England harbors where, as you walk down the length of the dock from harbor to shore for the first time, there is someone at the shore end with a smile, a handshake, and a welcome. I set off in the morning, but the wind is fresh and in my face. I return to harbor to stay another entire day. There is always plenty to do on the boat.

I tie up to a mooring at the back of the harbor where the water is calm and from under a bunk cushion pull the flat package I had stored there. Between the two firm panels of foam core is the artwork for LONDON's new lettering. Originally I lettered LONDON's name on her transom with simple small black block capitals I ordered from a marine discount store.

Over this past winter I e-mailed photos of the boat to a designer in Rhode Island. He e-mailed modified copies of the photos back to me. LONDON's name appeared lettered across her transom in a different style on each photo. I chose large red serif letters in a curved design with black shading to give them the appearance of depth. I will spend most of the day applying this artwork to the stern of the boat. First I get the dinghy tied across the stern. This is my scaffold.

I then use a scrub pad and cleanser to remove the old lettering. To apply the new letters I will *simply* need to peel off the backing and then rub them onto the clean hull surface. There is the matter of alignment. The letters are too large to apply in one big piece and need to be sliced into sections and then applied. I make some pencil marks on the white surface of the fiberglass transom to designate where various points of the pattern are to fall, wishing several times I had done this while the boat was still ashore. Even little waves are a nuisance when making marks that need to be precise. I begin applying the letters and find I cannot manage the sheet sliced even into two pieces, so I cut out and apply each letter individually. Once I have everything laid out in place with masking tape, I pull off the backing paper and begin to burnish the letters down. The results are credible, but to my eye not quite perfect. I think the leading *L* is a bit too low. However, later in the day I get talking to the launch driver about the lettering and how I think it is a bit askew. We discover we went to the same high school, the American School in London. He tells me these slight imperfections are the essence of character—and my transom looks fine.

I leave Scituate again the next morning as it is getting light in the east. The cockpit of the boat is wet with dew. I stand and steer among the quiet boats in the still harbor. LONDON's small diesel pushes us toward the glow of the old lighthouse. We clear the harbor jetties just as the sun comes up over Massachusetts Bay.

By 8:30 I'm making 3 to 4 knots in a light southeasterly breeze. The sails are up. The engine is off. I make this resolution: I am here to sail. I will avoid what a friend calls "gotta-get-there-itis." As long as I can make 2 knots of speed, the sails will stay up and the diesel off.

The day is clear and bright, the sea calm, quiet, and empty. LONDON just slips along in the sun as the coast drops further and further behind. I use the cockpit-mounted GPS to keep the boat aimed at that part of the horizon where the twin lighthouses on Thatcher Island off Cape Ann should appear. It is 10:30 before they come into view, and by then Scituate has slipped below the horizon behind me.

I use this calm time to install a forged stainless steel U-bolt in the sidewall of the cockpit. I quickly make two holes in the fiberglass with a cordless drill, seal their inside edges with silicone caulking, slip the threaded ends of the U-bolt through, install the steel backing plate, and then tighten the nuts. I now have a ring in my cockpit I can clip the tether of my harness to. I try it out. It is very solid.

Late in the morning a large tanker comes out of Boston in the main shipping lane. It quickly passes astern and over the horizon. The breeze has turned fitful by the time I approach Thatcher Island but freshens again after lunch. Lunch is my typical boat fare, hummus on pita bread with olives and tomato. The day becomes warm.

Approaching Rockport I spot a large charcoal-colored fin maybe three feet high flopping above the surface of the water and steer LONDON to get a closer look. I expect the fin to vanish at any moment, but it stays on the surface moving slowly forward. I maneuver my boat to sail close and parallel to this underwater monster, which I can now see below the surface of the water. It appears large, maybe 9 feet long, but cut off, as if the entire tail portion has been severed. There is no blood. It must be a mutilated shark or whale. An old wound perhaps. I leave a phone message describing what I've seen for the Rockport harbormaster as my path slowly diverges from the fish's.

I anchor LONDON in Sandy Bay off Rockport's Old Harbor. The entrance into the inner part of the harbor is now silted over for all but the smallest boats, but the huge blocks of granite are still firmly in place.

Later in the afternoon, swimming around LONDON, I look up to see a white fiberglass powerboat approach with a man and a woman aboard. They watch me as they cut the engine and glide in.

"Sure looks like you're having a good time."

I agree that I am. He and she continue to smile at me. I ask, "Why do I feel like this is leading somewhere?"

"Well . . . ," he says.

It turns out they are the Rockport harbormasters, Rosemary and Scott, and since I am already in the cold water, and if I would like to help—completely voluntary of course—there is a boat anchored just over there caught up in a lobster pot rope, and if I had a mask maybe I could dive underneath and see what I could see. I have a mask. It sounds like fun. I climb into their boat.

As we race over I look at the stricken sailboat. She is lying askew to her anchor line. It is a big boat. A man well dressed in blues and whites is pacing the cockpit. I get into the water again and swim under the boat. I can see a lot of old yellow polypropylene rope wrapped around the propeller. One end of the yellow potwarp descends steeply into the deep. The sailboat has one of those propellers that projects down under the hull, daring something to come along so the little bronze blades can grab at it, twist it around, play with it, and stop.

Back on the surface, the owner leans over and hands me a huge bowie knife. He looks me in the eye. He smiles. The blade must be a foot and a half long. It sparkles in the sun. I tread water while trying to cut through the rope with this frightening knife. It is incredibly dull. After splashing around in the water for a few minutes I finally pass a loop of rope and the knife back up to Scott, who saws away at the rope on his boat's gunwale until it finally parts. Swimming under the boat again, I am unable to untangle the rest of the line from the prop. They decide to go for a diver. On the ride back to my boat, Scott picks a lobster out of a pail of them in the boat. The lobster's unpegged claws snap.

"Here's your supper. Enjoy."

Back on board, I toss the lobster in the icebox and get some water boiling. The pot is too small, but I force the lobster in. There is no way he's going to fit. I hold him halfway down in the bubbling water with the pot lid. I don't let up until those little side legs stop kicking and begin to turn a bright red. By the time the lobster is ready, they are diving under the sailboat, and I watch out the companionway as I eat. There is no butter. It doesn't matter.

The small lobster claws always make me think of my grandmother. She was a tough little Scottish woman who would suck the meat out of each and every one of the thin side legs, while the rest of us, long done, stretched out our legs under the picnic table near the barn and watched her eat. When you had a lobster with Grandma, you took your time.

The night is calm, but with a rolling ocean swell. I sleep well.

In the morning, there is no wind. I motor out of Sandy Bay. A patchy mist lies on the gentle morning swell as LONDON chugs by the big green gong G3 that marks the western end of the old breakwater, mostly awash and sighing. Further to the east are the Dry Salvages. T.S. Eliot named the third of his *Four Quartets* after these rocks.

It is a quiet morning. The sea is glassy. A pod of pilot whales pass astern. By 8:00 A.M. Newburyport is abeam, and I can pick out some of the white steeples in the town behind the barrier island. Again I see a large floppy fin across the glassy sea. Yesterday I asked Rosemary about the strange fish I had seen approaching Rockport.

"An ocean sunfish."

I look it up later in the *Field Guide to North American Fishes*. The ocean sunfish, *Mola mola*, runs up to 13 feet long and has mirror-image dorsal and anal fins. The book describes it as shark-like, but with a rounded flap-like tail fin that looks cut off. *Mola* lies on its side on the surface to siphon in its food, which includes jellyfish, fish larvae, and squid. *Mola* can weigh 3,300 pounds, although specimens of about 500 pounds are more typical. It is an uncommon and peculiar fish. In *Fishes of the Gulf of Maine* it is reported that the sunfish's skin is unusually thick; the skin of one taken in August 1914 was measured at 1½ inches. That book also states that the fish may be luminescent at night and makes a grunting or groaning noise when caught[6]. With its big fin out of the water, looking like a miniature high-aspect sailing rig, this fish could almost sail if it could keep the fin from drooping as much as it does; there is another fin underneath, like a keel. According to the Smithsonian's book *SeaLife*, the fish is propelled by the "sculling motion" of the fins. It is listed along with the other bizarre fishes.

Soon the Isles of Shoals are visible directly ahead. I've traveled about 20 miles this morning and decide to stop at Star Island for lunch. Years ago my friend John and I talked of paddling my two-man kayak out here, but we never did. In *Among the Isles of Shoals* (1873), the poet Celia Thaxter describes the islands like this:

> Swept by every wind that blows, and beaten by the bitter brine for unknown ages, well may the Isles of Shoals be barren, bleak, and bare. At first sight nothing can be more rough and inhospitable than they appear. The incessant influences of wind and sun, rain, snow, frost and spray, have so bleached the tops of the rocks, that they look hoary as if with age, though in the summer-time a gracious greenness of vegetation breaks here and there the stern outlines, and softens somewhat their rugged aspect.

I pick up a mooring in Gosport Harbor and go ashore in the dinghy. A thin young woman in a bathing suit meets me on the dock, signs me in, and gives me a sheet of rules.

"The tour, which you must be interested in, begins at 1:30."

She first came here as a child and now works in the summer as one of the "Pelicans," who orient visitors to Star Island. She tells me the island is owned by Star Island Corporation and operated by them as a religious and educational conference center.

I walk up the slope toward the steps of the massive Oceanic Hotel, which dominates the landscape. Wooden screen doors swing and slap as people meander in happy groups on the huge wooden expanse of the hotel's porch. There are rocking chairs everywhere. The sound of voices singing old hymns floats from an open window a floor or two above me. Inside the old hotel the dining room is vast and empty, filled with large polished wooden tables set for lunch. Later, back on the boat, I hear a bell sound. Several hundred people gather on the slope of the lawn in front of the hotel.

The midday ferry from Portsmouth, New Hampshire pulls in. I drop the mooring, drift for a moment, and then start "Old Reliable" to make my way out of the harbor and pass west of Appledore Island, home of the Shoals Marine Laboratory field station[7]. Although there are moorings available for visitors, I am eager to be on my way north again. I set my sights on Cape Neddick, some 12 miles away.

I round the Cape Neddick lighthouse with its distinctive red light, turn to run along the northern shore of the neck, and slip into the granite walled slot off York Beach. I anchor here for the night in about 15 feet of water. I roll in the boat and listen to the crashing of surf on the beach. In the evening the sea settles down and I sleep.

When I leave in the morning fog is blowing in off the ocean. I pick my way through the lobster pots around Cape Porpoise and turn inland at Wood Island to stop at Biddeford Pool. A launch from the Biddeford Pool Yacht Club comes out to meet me and direct me to an available mooring. Even though it's early in the day, and I have only sailed 20 miles, I decide to stay over.

I shower at the yacht club and wander through the clubhouse looking at the pictures of generations of members posed in happy groups after sailboat races. I buy a lobster roll for lunch at an open-air restaurant up the hill from the yacht club. Across the street I load my backpack with groceries and ice. After a nap on the boat, I go ashore again for a walk and a swim on the ocean beach. The water is clear, light green in color, and surprisingly warm. I swim out and float on my back on the long ocean swells as they roll beneath me. I listen to the dull roar of the surf and look back to the long white Maine beach where I can see the French Canadian I met earlier. He seems still to be looking for his girlfriend. The spray from the break-ing waves produces a thin white haze, which blows inland into the thick green brush atop the dunes.

Later, back on LONDON, I meet another Cape Dory owner. I tell him about my adventure in Rockport. He relates how he snagged a whole line of lobster pots and dragged them in from the channel out near Wood Island all the way to his mooring without knowing it. It was only later when he could not get his engine into gear that he re-alized he had a tangle of rope around his prop and discovered his new string of traps.

Throughout this trip I would find lobster pots planted in channels regardless of how narrow the passage. At times the lobster buoys are so thick you wonder how there can be enough lobsters to fill them. You might also wonder if all these buoys, especially those in the channels, are placed there as a barrier to visiting boats. I certainly wish there were a clear passage 50 feet wide down the center of Maine's harbor channels. I would guess that the lobsters under this passage of clear water could scurry over to the tasty morsels in the traps lying on the edges of the channel, although somehow I doubt this is a popular view in Maine. I admit I am ignorant of the habits of lobsters.

I am grateful for the shape of my boat's hull. The full-keeled vessel presents few underwater obstructions to snag a passing line, and my propeller is safely tucked inside of the rudder and well above the base of the keel.

Continuing along the Maine coast I reach the Sheepscot River and sail up it to turn east into the narrow channel that leads to a quiet basin north of Sawyer Island. It is the beginning of Labor Day weekend when I pull into a small, completely enclosed cove. A seal and some herons standing on the mud watch me drop anchor.

After a quick red sunset, the mosquitoes come out in force, forcing me below, behind the protection of a sealed companionway and porthole screens. I spend a few hours below with supper and then some reading. After 10:00 I open the boat up again. The mosquitoes have vanished, as they often do later at night. I go on deck and look at the crescent moon. The cove is a dark polished surface; only the bark of a nearby dog disturbs the peace. Two lobster boats that flew in earlier with their hazy spotlights blazing are quiet now, moored nearby. The metal bridge rattles as a car roars over it and vanishes, playing its headlights through the pine trees. There are voices from a back porch. LONDON swings in the tidal current. A lobster boat bilge pump kicks on and runs for a minute or two, coughs, and stops. Something croaks in the marsh and a heron passes overhead with a hiss. I am definitely in Maine.

The next morning is the beginning of a series of cold, cloudy days. I leave Sawyer Island early and begin to motor the 9 more miles up the Sheepscot River toward the town of Wiscasset. I imagine a cup of fresh coffee and perhaps some pastry to supplement my daily diet of hummus, rice, and beans. The mackerel sky is gray. The water is still. There are many herons and seals. Green pine and spruce trees line the shoreline of the river above a band of cream granite. As I travel further north and upstream the river narrows and the lobster pots thicken. For the first time on the trip, lobstermen wave as I pass by, but a few miles south of Wiscasset, near a spot known as Colby Cove, I spin the boat around, kill the engine, and set the mainsail to run with the wind and current back down the Sheepscot: The lobster pots are too thick to risk going any further. I am afraid of getting the potwarps tangled in my propeller. There seems to be a pot every 4 or 5 feet.

Later in the day the wind comes up near the mouth of the river and I have an exciting sail out into Sheepscot Bay and back. With plenty of wind and no waves on this protected water, LONDON is soon flying along like an express train under all sail. That night I make it into Robinhood Cove, shower, do laundry, and feast on lobster pie at the Osprey Restaurant.

Several days later on my way home, about 3 miles before making the turn into Portsmouth, New Hampshire, my luck runs out. I am under full sail in an easterly breeze, heeled over a bit, when I hear the tap-tap of a lobster pot I did not see move along the hull. I come to a complete stop. I have snagged a potwarp off Sisters Point. I quickly loosen the sheets to let the sails flap, then drop the mainsail, and roll in the genoa.

In the clear water I can see the line holding me running at a 45-degree angle off the stern quarter. I am perhaps a mile off a rocky lee shore. The waves are choppy, but only 1 or 2 feet high. I push the line with my boathook. I pull at it. The wind and waves push the weight of the boat against the line. I can't move it.

I sit down to think what to do. The boat is bouncing up and down, slightly heeled over, sails and lines strewn about. I could jump in the water and cut the line, but I am alone. I am not sure about what would happen after the boat comes free. Would I be able to get back aboard easily? Probably. Even though I am not in any danger

I decide I will first let the Coast Guard know where I am. I also have the vague idea that if someone would pull me slightly upwind, the tension would come off the line and I could push it off and become unsnagged.

I call the Coast Guard on the VHF radio and they have me switch to my cell phone. I describe my location. We discuss my options and talk about where the line could be snagged on my boat. There are two possibilities. Since I was sailing with a bit of weather helm, my rudder was cocked a bit to one side. When the rudder is askew, a gap will open where the base of rudder meets the line of the keel bottom. It is not much of an opening, but maybe just enough. The other possibility is where the transducer for the depth finder sticks out on a teak stem. The Coast Guard suggests I power off. I am afraid to start the engine and possibly create a bigger tangle by wrapping the rope around the propeller shaft.

We talk on and off for maybe twenty minutes. During a gap in the conversation, the wind drops and then comes back shifted further south. To my surprise and relief, LONDON just floats free. I let the Coast Guard know, thank my lucky stars, get the sails back up, untangle the lines, and am under way again toward Portsmouth. I watch very carefully for lobster pots. I had been enjoying scooting along the coast looking at the shore, but now I travel a bit further out.

It is late afternoon when I grab a yacht club mooring in Kittery's Pepperrell Cove. A yacht club launch pulls up with a young woman at the controls. She passes me a clipboard and circles in the launch while I sit down in the cockpit to fill out the form for a mooring rental. I hear the launch's engine die, look up, and then go back to the forms. The launch engine starts again, struggles, and dies again. The starter grinds a few more times and then it is quiet.

"Oh phooey! Can you help me?"

I look up at her standing in the launch maybe 150 feet away. I am reminded somehow of my own daughters.

"It's only my second day."

She is adrift. A line trailing from the launch has wrapped around

and tangled her propeller. I climb into my inflatable making little
groaning sounds, pull at the outboard and zip over to where she is
drifting toward the beach. I get her rafted up alongside another boat
moored nearby, warn her about getting her fingers between the
bouncing boats, and get her to call the other yacht club launch to
come to her rescue. We get bumpers in position between the boats
and wait. Once assistance arrives, I slip away to go ashore on the
Kittery side for groceries and ice and then a hot shower.

That night, before I fall asleep in my bunk, I draw a sketch in my
journal of a little winged flange I could make for the bottom of the
keel. It is to guide a rope past the gap near the rudder. I think about
switching to an in-hull transducer for the depth finder. While I am
doing this, a heron passes overhead with a croak. Herons, I understand, are a sign of good luck.

8

A Canal Cockpit

Leaving Portsmouth Harbor I pass Whaleback Light on a heading to pass west of the Isles of Shoals. I put the boat on autopilot, settle down in the cockpit, and read Conrad for the rest of the morning.

As I approach Cape Ann the breeze begins to build. I toss the book below and am soon busy with the boat as I push upwind to get into position to tack around Cape Ann. At 2:00 P.M. I make the turn and fly along under full sails, in foul-weather gear and a lot of wind. I clear the Londoner, but have trouble controlling the boat in the building wind. There is too much weather helm. I head up and reef the mainsail. The boat settles right down, sailing faster and easier. I anchor off Salem, Massachusetts in the shelter of Great Misery Island for the night.

As the evening light deepens a steady stream of powerboats pull in and out of the cove on cruises out of nearby Beverly and Salem. Police and harbormaster boats from the local towns hover a bit further off. I watch the red and green lights idle by. Engines sputter, softened by laughter as darkness falls.

Twice the next day I try to make some headway against the fresh wind, but both times I give up and go back behind Great Misery to wait for calmer weather. The forecast is not good. It's becoming clear I won't make it back to Fairhaven this weekend. I absolutely need to be at work on Monday. I have an inspiration: I decide to sail up into Salem Harbor and leave the boat there for a week. I will

LONDON at Sea

return the following weekend and finish the trip. This also means I will get to see my wife, Nancy, a few days earlier.

I head toward Salem Harbor. The wind grows stronger. Gusts make black agitated patches on the surface of the water, whipping the tops off the little waves. There is a flapping sound. My mainsail has torn. I drop the sail before it rips any further. It has blown out around the lower batten pocket. Once on a mooring at Salem, I take the sail off and pack it up in a sailbag to take ashore. In the evening I catch the harbor launch to shore and wait for my wife near the remains of Derby Wharf.

Derby Wharf was the heart of old Salem in the 1790s. It was from here that ships sailed for the East and West Indies, making Salem for a time the sixth-largest city in the United States[8]. The area around Derby Street was lined with sailmaking lofts, ship chandlers, warehouses, and counting houses. Spars and rigging would have been strewn about the ground and wharves. New ships were built nearby for the East Indian trade. The harbor was crowded with ships sailing to and from China, Calcutta, Cádiz, Lisbon, the West Indies, and all the U.S. ports. These ships would have carried sailcloth, rum, wine, oil, lemons, raisins, coffee, cocoa, molasses, sugar, salt, tea, spices, and many other cargoes in the rich and prosperous trade. Today there is a park and a marina here with condos and restaurants. You can still walk out onto the old wharf.

The sailbag containing LONDON's torn main sits next to me on the sidewalk. Cars rush by. I see the familiar red car and hop in.

At home I buy a small square of sailcloth over the Internet and use Nancy's sewing machine to stitch a reinforcement panel around the torn batten. The following Saturday Nancy drives me back to Salem Harbor at dawn. I hoist my newly repaired main and sail out to round the rocks at Great Haste and skim across Salem Sound. The rail is bubbling in the water as I move toward Marblehead Neck and then out into Massachusetts Bay.

It is blowing 25 knots again, but more from the west. I am rested and ready. I make steady progress again. As darkness falls I make my

way into Plymouth Harbor, some 50 miles across Massachusetts Bay
from Salem. Although I need to motor up the channel against the
tide, into a brisk headwind and the glare of the setting sun, I go all
the way into Plymouth's inner harbor. It is a windy night and I don't
fancy spending it at anchor in a less sheltered spot. My fingers are
stiff with cold when I grab a mooring in the last of the day's light.
The replica of the original MAYFLOWER is tied near shore, perhaps
100 yards from my mooring. From Salem to Plymouth: I am sailing
through the heart of Massachusetts maritime history.

Chilled through, I go below, cook supper, and eat quickly. Later,
sitting on my bunk, with the cabin closed up against the cold night,
I look over my log for the day. At 9:00 in the morning I cleared the
red-green buoy off Marblehead and turned toward Cohasset. By
10:30 I was abeam of Boston Buoy, which floats 16 nautical miles
east of Boston, and I was off the Scituate sea buoy by 2:00 P.M. Here
the wind became fitful for an hour, but then came on strong again
from the west. By 5:15, I was at the lighthouse on the sandy bluff
known as the Gurnet Point off Plymouth, where I started the engine. The surface of the sea had been agitated all day. I climb into
my sleeping bag pleased with the day's progress.

Later, as I sit at my desk at home rewriting this passage on a dark
November evening, I will check conditions at that very same Boston
Buoy I sailed past using the NOAA weather site on the Internet. At
10 P.M., the wind speed at Boston Buoy (or old 44013, as she is af-
fectionately known) is 23.3 knots, with gusts to 27 knots, out of the
north-northeast. The waves are 8.5 feet every six seconds and the
barometric pressure is 29.92 and falling rapidly. The air temperature is 48°F and the water temperature is 46°F. An 8-foot wave is the
height of the average living room wall. If one of these passes every
six seconds, it takes a brief three seconds to slide from the peak of
one wave down into the trough, and another three seconds to climb
to the top of the next crest. These are steep waves. There is little
recreational sailing done around here in November.

When I wake in Plymouth Harbor I hop out of my warm sleeping bag, turn on the marine weather forecast, and hop right back in

to listen. Again windy weather is predicted. I will raise my sail in the inner harbor and set it reefed. It can be tricky to get the main up in wind while sailing alone—especially in a confined place like this harbor. I start the engine and use the auto-tiller to head the boat into the wind on a slow sputtering course diagonally across the main channel, and climb out of the cockpit onto the cabintop to reef and raise the main. Before we reach the shallows on the other side I scramble back into the cockpit, take the tiller from the autopilot, spin the boat to fall off before the wind, and reach down and kill the engine. A good autopilot makes these single-handed maneuvers much easier.

With the wind and the tide behind me, I fly across the choppy water of Massachusetts Bay, often heeled well over, making 6.5 knots over the ground. I reach the entrance of the Cape Cod Canal too early; there is more than an hour's wait for the tide to turn. LONDON's 8-hp engine lacks the power to push the boat much against the strong flood current still pouring out of this end of the canal. It is better to wait. I linger near the beach, heaved-to in the gusty wind, and cook a hot lunch which I eat in the cockpit while watching the sport fishermen trolling back and forth off Scusset Beach. I am close enough to the beach to smell the pitch pines ashore. The wind rocks LONDON from side to side.

While waiting I study the canal entrance on the shore. Big breakwaters stick out into the bay. A power plant with a big stack abuts the canal just inside the entrance. Otherwise the land is low and flat. I try to imagine the scene before the canal was dug. There were originally two small rivers reaching toward one another across the narrow sandy isthmus that separated Cape Cod Bay and Buzzards Bay. The Monument River flowed south into Buzzards Bay, while the Scusset flowed northeasterly into Cape Cod Bay. Although the first canal was opened in 1914, its construction had been proposed by Miles Standish of the Plymouth Colony, who traveled up the Scusset River and then portaged to the Monument in 1623.

Before the canal, ships traveling up the coast had to go around the outside of Cape Cod. They sailed through Vineyard Sound, past

Vineyard Haven, and across Nantucket Sound and then either northeast through Pollock Rip Channel or east through Great Round Shoal Channel before turning north to run up along the long beach on the outside of Cape Cod. It was a treacherous and busy route. In the 1790s, 50 or 60 vessels could be seen at one time at places along this route. It is estimated that 120 ships a day rounded the cape during the 1860s. There were many shipwrecks. Between 1875 and 1903, nearly 700 ships were wrecked on the Outer Cape. During wartime shipping was vulnerable. The British Navy harassed shipping during the Revolution and the War of 1812. In 1918, during WWI, a German U-boat attacked a tug pulling barges off Chatham. The barges were sunk[9].

When the Cape Cod Canal was first opened on July 29, 1914, it was in the hands of a private company. It was also narrower and shallower than it is today. Traffic was one-way. The company charged tolls but failed to make money. Much of the shipping up and down the coast still chose to go outside the cape, fearing the narrow channel and swift currents. After being taken over by the government, the canal was improved to become the huge, broad ditch it is today. There is still current in the canal. The water swirls and bubbles. The average maximum ebb current is about 4.5 knots.

My trip through the canal is uneventful at first. I enter at the end of the flood and slowly move against the dying current. As time passes the flood peaks and the current begins to swing and swirl, to idle uncertainly around the boat before beginning the ebb, to pour back through the canal, in an inevitable building rush toward Buzzards Bay. I am running under power, as is required, but have left the mainsail up sheeted in tight to help where it can. As the wind begins to build from directly ahead, it luffs the main with a snapping ferocity. I drop and furl the old sail before it rips again. Small waves begin to run down the canal toward me, and the wind tears off their tops, forming long white streaks across the choppy surface. Along the banks of the canal, fishermen are pulling in their lines and leaving. Aluminum beach chairs blow over. The trees sway this way and that. I am moving faster now toward the big southern bay under control of the growing tidal current. As the railroad bridge over the canal comes into view, spray is beginning to fly over the boat. I have donned my slicker. Incredibly, the wind continues to strengthen.

Under the railroad bridge itself, in the last few miles of the southern end of the canal, the wind and the tide running against one another have created an impressive mess. The waves are green, steep, and breaking. LONDON's bow plows through each wave top and then plunges deep into each trough. The boat gives a shudder and does it again. I am convinced that during some of these descents into the troughs my propeller is actually out of the water, as the entire boat seems to shake *from stem to stern*. People walking along the side of the canal, leaning into the wind, begin to stare and point at me. I find this nerve-racking but hang on as best I can in the heaving cockpit. It is too late to get my harness from below and clip in. The motion becomes increasingly violent.

I am stuck. I can't turn around and go back. I doubt I have the horsepower to make much way against the current. I can only go forward into the wind and building sea, using the engine to keep her nose into the waves. The waves get bigger. One wave swings LONDON crosswise in a roll. I rev the engine to full throttle and struggle to swing her nose back into the waves. I decide to call the Cape Cod Canal Control; I have the handheld VHF in my pocket. One hand for the tiller, one for the radio, I press my legs across the cockpit to hold me in. I feel a strong urge to be somewhere else, but I force myself to be calm. I explain my situation over the radio. I tell them I think I am reaching my boat's limits. I ask for advice on the first place where I can turn out of the canal.

The voice from Canal Control directs me toward the channel to the town of Onset, tells me that the swells aren't that bad, and, most helpfully, suggests I run down the side of the channel where the waves will be smaller when I get to the area where the canal opens up. I thank him and sign off. Talking to someone has made me feel better.

The radio squawks and I hear that another sailboat in the canal, a quarter mile from where I am, has just lost her mast. She is said to be in trouble. A siren goes off at the rescue station behind me and one of the deep-V-shaped canal boats flies by with sirens and flashing lights. As it passes, a crewman looks down at me lolling in a trough from his position high above on a neighboring wave crest. He turns forward and says something to his companion, and they roar away into the now-screaming wind. The pessimist in me thinks it must be, "We'll be back for this one in a minute." The optimist hears, "That's a Cape Dory. A real sea boat. He'll be fine." These little dialogues keep me amused while I wait to get sucked out of here and into the open water.

It is a matter of hanging on, racing past the dismasted sailboat on the opposite bank, and keeping the bow into the waves. Once I am out of the narrowest part of the canal I work my way over to the edge. Here the canal opens up and begins to calm down.

Once I make the right turn into the Onset side channel it is calm and warm. I stretch with relief and strip off layers of clothing. I find a place in Onset to anchor and drop the big CQR. The wind whips across the harbor. On the weather radio I hear there are now gale warnings posted for Buzzards Bay. I decide to spend the night where I am.

It is mid-afternoon. I have plenty of time to look through the galley for something new to cook. I fill the frying pan with olive oil, roll falafel balls out of a batter mix, and cook them in the hot oil. I have tomatoes and plain yogurt. The leftovers will make tomorrow's pita sandwich.

I would guess the waves in the canal were no more than 6 feet high, but steep. These are not like the waves out at Boston Buoy in November, which are built by the wind racing across a long fetch of water. In the canal, the current running against the wind builds the waves. The experience in the canal was less like sailing and more like riding a fat, heavy raft with a big mast down a swift river.

The next day I finish the trip to my mooring. The mainsail tears again in a gust off Mattapoisett. I pull it down. The rip is around a different batten pocket. I sail the last few miles with the genoa alone, the first time I have done this on LONDON. I am surprised at how balanced the boat is, how well she sails the rest of the way to Fairhaven.

It has been an eventful trip up to Maine's Sheepscot River and back, full of firsts, full of excitement. I was never in any real danger, but I have snagged my boat on a line for the first time, torn my sail for the first and the second time, spoken to the Coast Guard for the first time, and Canal Control too. I remind myself I have also helped the harbormasters in Rockport and a launch driver in Portsmouth.

I get off the boat in Fairhaven and go home completely satisfied—on top of the world.

9

Winter 2000–2001

The scene is grim when Bruce and I meet at the marina on the morning of November 1. He has kindly come to help me again bring the boat in. The wind is coming in out of the northeast at 25 knots. It is cloudy. Cold salt spray flies over us as we motor out to LONDON. I ease the inflatable toward the boat while watching Bruce time his grab at the teak rail as the stern swings across our path. My legs are wet and cold. I have left my foul-weather gear on the boat, so it doesn't do me much good on the way out to the boat.

We have a little time before our appointment with the crane. We start by sliding the mainsail out of the mast track and off the boom. We stuff it into the cabin out of the wind. I will fold it later. We stuff the working jib into the forward hatch as LONDON lurches under us in the choppy water. Then I yell through the wind to Bruce that we'll do the rest at the dock. He unties us from the mooring and we motor toward the boatyard's crane.

To get to the crane we head for the road that runs atop the stone causeway and then turn into the little channel that runs parallel to it. We are 50 feet away from the road surface and just below eye level with it. A car races by out to the island. I see the driver look down from his car window at Bruce standing on LONDON's bow. I steer around the end of the long dock, leaving astern the sound of tires whining across the causeway. We make another turn and slide into the little stone slip adjacent to the crane. One of the crew is there to catch our lines. I kill the engine. Another season is over.

At this marina, as at many, the boatowner is expected to work with the crew to get the rigging loose and unstep the mast. Dave comes on board, looks over our disorganized, half-finished mess, and gives us instructions. He only has a few hours to use this slot on every tide. There are other boats to come out after us today. We take the boom off and wedge it in the cabin. The crane roars into life. A puff of black diesel smoke lifts into the air. As the crane's strap is fastened around the mast, Bruce and I begin loosening the turnbuckles of the inner shrouds and then the outers, the backstay, and finally the difficult one—a cotter pin at the end of a clevis pin that holds the tangs of the roller-furler headstay to the stemhead fitting. We coil the halyard lines neatly against the mast, and with another roar of the crane and another puff of black smoke, the mast lifts up to float in the air before being slowly lowered down and laid across the bow pulpit, the cabintop, and the stern rails. Then we straighten up the cabin, put the tools away, and get everything tied down for the 80-mile journey LONDON is about to take down the interstate on the back of a truck. Finally I close her up and hop off the boat.

LONDON *Lifted*

Two huge straps are now floated under LONDON. On the first attempt to lift her she gets may be 3 feet in the air when the forward strap slides toward the bow and she splashes back into the water. Dave yells from the crane cabin at the dockhand and they try it again. This time it is a good lift. The crane swings her up and out of the water at around 90 degrees so she is hovering over the roadway. They tie a line from amidships to the crane base so she won't float around in the breeze.

While her hull is power-washed clean of the season's growth of slime, I unfasten the outboard from the inflatable and hand it up to Bruce waiting on the dock. The outboard goes in the back of my van. The inflatable will go on the truck with LONDON after the barnacles are blown off by the power-washer. Her bottom thoroughly cleaned, LONDON is set on the bed of a truck trailer and strapped down. We load the rest of the gear into the van and drive off. I will meet the truck in another two hours at my house so I can be sure LONDON is left where I want her for the winter.

I have a list of things to do this winter to bring LONDON to the next stage of her restoration, but first comes the end of season cleanup and winterizing. This must be done before the cold weather sets in.

When the truck arrives at my house Bill hops down from the cab and looks around at all the woods. "I can see why you like it down by our place. It is about as different as can be from here."

He takes the big wood blocks off the truck and carefully positions them under the forward and aft ends of the long keel. He accidentally takes a step back onto the paw of my rottweiler mutt, Maya, who jumps back with a yelp and then lurches forward to lick his hand.

"Friends for life, eh mutt?"

Bill gets the five tripod stands in position and then uses the truck's hydraulic arms to lower the boat onto them. As he is doing this he tells me he is retiring. His son Dave will be running the business next season. We talk till he's done and the big truck pulls away.

After he's gone, I finish my lunch and then hurry off to work. I am at my desk by 2:00.

————— ∞∞∞ —————

By November 19 I have emptied, winterized, and covered the boat. The dinghy has been washed and stowed, and the outboard has been flushed and mounted on a rack in our cellar furnace room where it should be free from freezing temperatures.

I winterize the diesel with the garden hose. First I string the hose across the yard and into the boat. I screw onto the end of the hose a fitting I have made that terminates in a ½-inch hose barb. I pull the Yanmar's raw water cooling line off the seawater filter and push it onto the hose barb, clamp it, and open the hose faucet about halfway to allow only moderate pressure. I start the diesel. I want the engine to warm up. I am going to change the oil too. While standing in the cockpit watching as the diesel putts on, spraying puffs of fresh water and exhaust gases from her stern, I decide to put it in gear. There is a rattling and shaking as the screw begins to rotate. I put it in neutral and then try again. Much too much vibration. I put it back in neutral, climb down the ladder out of the cockpit, and walk under the stern where I can reach the propeller. I grab it and wiggle it. It feels loose.

A few days later I call the boatyard. Dave thinks the cutless bearing is probably gone. When I hear him say it I know he's right—the bearing was twenty-three years old and already loose. I ask him to pick up the boat earlier than planned in the spring. They will replace the bearing for me in Fairhaven. I have always had too much water coming in where the shaft exits the boat, having never been able to get the old stuffing box properly adjusted. Replacing the cutless bearing will mean all this gets rebuilt. I will finally have a dry boat.

On March 17, 2001, I take the backstay to the rigger to be replaced with a new one. The headstay was done last year. Back at home I dig a path through the 18 inches of snow out to the boat, brush the snow off the tarp, and pull the tarp back so I can move around in the cockpit. I carry the trickle charger up the ladder and hook it up to battery number two. Then I go below and remove the head. I replace it with a new one of an identical model. It is a good day to do this: There is a breeze and the air is cold. I tried using the rebuild kit last year, but the head still leaked. This will be the solution. I should no longer have that little dribble of water running down my cabin sole.

Today is both St. Patrick's Day and Evacuation Day. Evacuation Day is a local holiday that marks the day in 1776 during the Revolutionary War when the British left Boston for the remainder of the war. They were by this time surrounded. The cannons brought overland from Fort Ticonderoga had been placed on the Dorchester Heights, making their situation even more perilous. The British Fleet was allowed to leave in peace as the British in turn promised not to burn Boston. More than 100 warships and transports carrying some 10,000 soldiers and loyalists set sail for Halifax less than a year after the battles of Lexington and Concord. I could get off my boat right here, walk into the woods, and keep going for about 4 miles. I would come out of the woods near North Bridge in Concord, where the fighting started. It would be as far inland as the British ever got around here.

The new mainsail arrives this week. It will replace the one that ripped twice at the end of the season. I also plan to add a new sail cover made from the same brown Sunbrella fabric I used for the dodger last season.

The next day I switch the trickle charger over to battery number one, check the operation of all the seacocks, and remove the old gasket from the forward hatch, which has begun to leak. I now need to find a half-round gasket for a 20-inch square hatch. A week later I order a new depth meter with an in-hull, puck-style transducer.

On March 24 I make a gasket from some old hose that is soft and of the correct diameter. It feels like a chubby, black snake as I feed and press it into the groove, but after I have it fitted the hatch will not close properly. I pull my work apart and clean the dried silicone out of the groove.

So the day will not be entirely wasted I clean up some of the wiring on the mast, installing a new connector plug, and check all the bulbs with my digital voltmeter. In this and the other electrical work I do, Nigel Calder's *Boatowners's Mechanical and Electrical Manual* is my guide.

On the last day of the month I drive over to Peabody to pick up my new backstay; I also get 20 feet of new ⁵⁄₁₆-inch anchor chain and some big shackles.

I knock the new snow off the boat cover and pull it back so the decks will dry faster in the sun. It is a nice day, cool and sunny, a day when you feel spring is near. The days are getting longer. Today the sun will not set till 6:08, and daylight savings time starts tomorrow. Up on deck, high above the ground, if I stop moving and listen I can hear the white-throated sparrows calling out "Old Sam Peabody, Peabody, Peabody!" I begin the installation of the new depth finder.

By the end of the day on April 14, I have the depth finder in and have also replaced the gasket in the forward hatch with one that fits. The next day, before I reassemble the berth I have taken apart to install the depth finder, I cut and install a top-access hatch to the under-bunk storage. To protect the transducer puck, which intrudes up into the under-bunk locker, I fit it with a cover I make from a flexible plastic bowl I find in the kitchen. I cut an exit slot for the wire and use a sheet metal screw to fasten it directly to the fiberglass liner.

Boat pickup is scheduled for May 10. Before the truck comes I repaint the boot stripe a bright red, spot-sand and paint the bottom with antifouling paint, spot-sand the teak and apply Cetol, wrap the spreader ends with new sail tape, and permanently install a new tube-shaped radar reflector in the shrouds.

The cutless bearing replacement is expensive but well worth it. I have a drier boat. This is one job I am happy to pay someone else to do and they do excellent work.

LONDON's mast is stepped by the same crane that pulled it off.

There is a bit of a hitch when I go to start the engine to pull away out to the mooring. No power. After a bit of searching we find the engine ground had been disconnected during the work and not re-attached. Dave fixes this for me and I start the engine. As we pull out of the slip I feel a bump as we touch the bottom but keep going. The tide is falling. We finish up hanking on the sails and the other launch-day chores while tied to another section of dock in much deeper water.

At the end of the summer I plan to go to Maine again. Early in July, Nancy and I are planning to meet the Cape Dory fleet further south at Coecles Harbor on the eastern end of Shelter Island. It lies between the two forks of Long Island, New York. I am looking forward to this cruise. We will also go to Block Island and Napatree with the Cape Dorians, as a fleet.

I've sailed to Coecles before on a chartered boat named THE RE-PUBLIC OF VERMONT. It is a beautiful place. I well remember the shallow entrance. The stream runs right out through the beach. You have to pick your way in but once inside there is an easy, protected anchorage. Much of the anchorage is surrounded by the Mashomack Nature Preserve, more than 2,000 acres of protected land with osprey and many other birds and a rare pine swamp area with floating sphagnum moss. When I was there with my sister, we watched deer carefully making their way along a causeway to the west, silhouetted by the evening sky.

We were no sooner anchored that night than we turned on the radio and heard a major change in the weather forecast. A hurricane that had been stalled much further south had changed direction and was now predicted to pass over us in forty-eight hours. We did elect to stay there that night, trying to sleep as thunderstorms raced through the hot night, one after another, with tremendous bangs. In the morning we set off early to get back to our berth. A sailboat that had attempted to enter during the night was aground at the side of the entrance channel.

By late afternoon we were back at our dock in downtown Mystic, Connecticut. The following day, still uncertain about the path of the hurricane, we spent the day at Mystic Seaport. I am a bit of a maritime museum junkie. The sight of an old clipper hull will cause my daughters to emit sighs and groans.

"Can't you just leave us at the hotel? Dad! Are you listening to me?"

Actually, I am not. Mystic Seaport is one of the great museums for the maritime enthusiast, with its ships, small boats, workshops and sail lofts.

The storm decided not to move after all. We went sailing again— this time to anchor at Napatree, which was so torn up by the hurricane in 1938. I kept a nervous eye to the south and on the sky.

10

Rendezvous Missed

Fifteen miles off the shore of southern New England my wife Nancy is setting up the scrabble board on the bridge deck. It is a beautiful Sunday morning in July. Rhode Island Sound is unusually clear and cool. Visibility seems unlimited. I look up at the silver boom swaying a foot over my head. The boom lifts slightly, the sail fills to the curved shape of an airfoil, and then the boom drops as the wind dies and the sail flattens. The water sparkles. We are moving sedately at about 2 to 2.5 knots, just a bit slower than a quick walker. I adjust our course and trim our sails for maximum effect in the light wind.

Our goal seems farther away as the day progresses. This is the reality of sailing: Sometimes you don't get anywhere. We are heading into the prevailing wind, so not only are we moving slowly, but we are tacking back and forth—drawing a zigzag course across the surface of the ocean toward where we want to go. A friend once described tacking to me as "traveling further than you ever imagined, to arrive where you want to be later than you thought possible."

When I daydream about sailing, our next cruise appears in a kind of amber light, where the wind is blowing at a steady 17 knots and from a convenient direction. I forget how the day's wind will often go from too little to too much. There is this rolling breach between sailing reality and my salty but gentle dreams.

This trip began while the boat was on her stands in the yard surrounded by a sea of snow and we used our computer to mon-

itor the California Cape Dory Owners Association website
(http://www.toolworks.com/capedory/) for this week's plans.
Nancy and I are on our way to meet a group of people we only
know from the Internet. Like us, they all own Cape Dory sailboats. We are to rendezvous with the Northeast Fleet at Coecles
Harbor on Shelter Island on Tuesday. Yesterday we left our home
marina in Fairhaven with a moderate and favorable breeze.
Within an hour it turned to blow hard in our faces. It would continue for the rest of the afternoon. All afternoon we tack up the
bay, at times with a reef in the main and the sea washing across
the decks, until we drop anchor at Cuttyhunk at 7:30 P.M.

Cuttyhunk is crowded with cruising sailboats. We don't even try
to go into the pond; we watched the forest of masts in the harbor
growing thicker during our long afternoon slog upwind. We anchor
way out where the bottom is stony with the big CQR. When it is
dark we see bonfires blazing on the beach and little figures moving
from the dome of flickering light into the dark. Years ago, when I
was here with Nancy on the Fourth of July, I carefully explained to
her how these fires were used by the islanders for a little-known annual ritual. Once the bonfire was lit and blazing well, the islanders
would begin the dark, repetitive chant, "Burn the runt, burn the
runt . . ." Then the smallest sailboat found that night in the harbor
was pulled onto shore, lifted from the water by hundreds of eager
hands, and tossed upon the flames to wild cries of excitement and
joy. Only this sacrifice would ensure the safety of the remainder of
the sailing fleet for the season. And, I explained, we were that boat!
It was then that she socked me in the arm. A 27-foot boat has become small in these waters. Most people, it seems, need something
larger.

Lying in my berth that night I again hear the noise from what I
think of as "underwater woodpeckers." I have been unable to find
out what creatures make this noise. I often hear them at night in
Buzzards Bay or Vineyard Sound. A staccato tapping heard through
the hull, never on deck. It is an underwater sound. One creature
taps for two to four seconds. Then from a different direction, and

often further away, another one answers. Back and forth, taps are exchanged and then silence. I forget about it. It starts again.

In the morning I raise anchor before the 5:00 A.M. sunrise and, huddled in the dewy cockpit sipping tea, navigate past Penikese Island and on out of Buzzards Bay. The day starts with a good and favorable breeze from the west, but as the morning wears on it shifts to the south and softens. It has blown all night from the west. We should have sailed last night, but I was just too lazy and tired, as I often am on the first day out. It takes a day or two of cruising to build up my energy and endurance.

We roll gently across the long ocean swells, the *groundswell*. Delicious translucent blue waves move under LONDON with quiet strength. The sun grows warm on our skin but there is still a cool freshness to the day. The swells are from a low-pressure system way out in the Gulf Stream. A gentle rise goes on and on, and then from the peak of the swell we begin the long settle into the trough. These are huge waves, but there is such a long interval between them that one hardly notices them. It is often like this out on the Sound. The power of the open Atlantic is undiminished by any barrier, shoal, or island. I had been out here in this same cockpit on a day like this two years ago when I had the same feeling I have now. I strip and laze for an hour in the sun before rigging the solar shower from the aluminum boom. I sit under it on the floor of the cockpit and wash in very little warm fresh water. Nancy showers after me. We begin that game of scrabble dry and clean.

The arrangement of letters on the board is soon driven by our competition into a tight, unevenly balanced pattern skewed to one side of the board that neither of us can make much more out of. I go below for a moment to plot our position from the GPS onto the big chart of Rhode Island Sound. I see the same tight pattern, the limited choices, on the chart. We are being pinched further and further out to sea as we head as close to the wind as we can. On a starboard tack, with Block Island off our starboard bow, we will have to go a lot further out to get the tack angle we need to make the passage near the island's north reef. I don't want to go that far out, or sail that long today. So we tack now, on a course that will take us across the entrance to Newport and around to Dutch Harbor, on the back side of Jamestown. Nancy pictures dinner in Jamestown, the hot showers at the Dutch Harbor boatyard, and is happy.

After an early lunch, she takes a nap below and then I do, with her taking the watch, so that when I come on deck it is mid-afternoon and we are approaching four fleets of sailboats racing off Newport. The first group we pass astern. With their stiff foil sails they seem like giant dark moths fluttering toward the shore. Opposite, on the ocean side, are fifty colorful spinnakers hovering like delicious lollipops on a calm sea—strawberry and lime, grape and lemon with swirls. I put the motor on to get past their downwind mark before the race arrives. Then I cut the engine and we glide out of our spurt of speed to watch each boat drop its colored bag and put up a plain triangular foresail to go upwind.

We pull into Dutch Harbor and grab a mooring about 4:30. I take a peek in the engine compartment. The white catch basin under the diesel is full of oil that must have leaked out of "Old Reliable" today. I close it up again, leaving the mess for the morning, hop in the dinghy with Nancy, and give her a big smile. We zoom off to shore and then take the walk across the peninsula to the town of Jamestown on the other side. The neighborhood we pass through is old and quiet. Many houses have extravagant flower gardens. Laughter drifts off warm screen porches in the green of the evening.

In the morning, while Nancy goes for ice, I clean the mess up and run the engine for a time. No more oil leaks. We will continue our voyage.

We ghost down the West Passage and out into the Sound in the company of three other boats. I set the auto-tiller and Nancy and I settle down to another game of scrabble as we slide along shore, moved more by the outgoing tide than the wind, jibing occasionally to work our way out. At the mouth of the river the wind dies completely and we motor for fifteen minutes, out to where I can see the water is ruffled, rippled with a new breeze, the first hint of the afternoon southwester. I kill the engine and begin to tack out between the draggers working this area. One fishing boat moves across our bow, leaving behind a wake filled with floating seagulls. We jibe in their midst and they flutter up around the sail as it slowly swings over the cockpit.

The breeze freshens through the afternoon. By the time we are about an hour from the entrance to Block Island Harbor it is nearly 6:00 P.M. The GPS is giving me an ETA of 6:50, 6:55, 6:40 depending on our speed at that instant. It has gotten rough. Nancy is seasick and in the bunk below. The wind blows against the tide just inside the North Reef. On a fast reach we leap off one wave to slam into the next. The bow lifts up and then falls down, spray flies through the air. I am soaked through, but the water is warm. I plotted my turn onto this tack perfectly, and we are now running for the entrance to Great Pond at Block Island at 182 degrees magnetic. I am happy and filled with a navigational satisfaction. I know where I am. I know where I am going. For now it is everything.

By the time we are inside the Block Island's Great Salt Pond and searching for a spot to anchor it is after 7:00 in the evening.

In three long days we have covered 65 miles on our route to Block Island: eight hours of sailing Saturday, twelve on Sunday, and another ten or so today. Nancy wants a day off. I agree. We settle down to enjoy the island, but I am worried. We are moving too slowly toward the gathering of our fellow Cape Dorians. We will be pinched for time. Our youngest daughter arrives in Boston on Friday and we absolutely have to be at the airport to meet her. It is now Monday night. We are anchored in 7.2 feet of water in Great Pond with the tide half out. We are tight on the depth too. I figure at low water we will have a foot or two of water under the keel.

I question what I could have done better. Perhaps I should have stayed the course on Sunday and not gone in to Jamestown. We might have been here a day earlier. We decide to give up on reaching Coecles Harbor and now plan to meet the Cape Dory fleet as they move eastward toward us at Napatree, an easy sail from here. We can be there on Wednesday evening. Tuesday will be a day off to enjoy Block Island. Wednesday we will anchor with the Cape

Dory fleet and then take off mid-morning on Thursday to push back to Fairhaven; with the prevailing southwest wind behind us, this should be no problem.

We wake to the cry, "Coffee on board! Coffee on board!" The bakery boat! I call him on the VHF. He finds us way over on the edge of the moored boats, and we buy coffee and fresh blueberry turnovers to begin the day. In town I buy two T-shirts, each with a single Chinese character printed on it, one for *courage*, the other *truth*—or at least that's what the English translation on the back of the shirt reads. I could be walking around with the Chinese character for "idiot" on my chest. I would not know. When I show the shirts to my daughter later in the week, she will say, "Oh Dad! They are so cheesy!" We swim, we nap, we walk around, we eat out. A perfect day on Block.

When sailing I am obsessed with weather forecasts. I will listen to them on the VHF over and over until I have built up the complete picture in my mind: Where the fronts are, what the conditions are across New England, what the wind strength will be and from what direction. I go through this on Wednesday morning. The forecast now, from our perspective, is pretty bad. It will blow from the northeast for the next two days with increasing strength. So much for sailing home on the prevailing southwesterly in time to pick up Laura. I can't take a chance on missing her. We decide to turn and run, even though it means giving up on any chance of meeting the Cape Dory fleet this season.

When we get out there, we find the wind has come round to the southeast. After we round the North Reef, we settle in on a long, 25-mile reach at 85 to 90 degrees magnetic. Near the end of this tack, at the mouth of Buzzards Bay and late in the afternoon, when the waves have built up enough for me to go below, moving around my again-prone wife, to find my harness to clip into the cockpit, the wind suddenly drops and then just as quickly comes up strong out of the northeast. We have just been given the opportunity to tack our way home against the wind and the outgoing tide. Soon there is a cross sea running, waves from the old and the new wind direc-

tions combining with the tide washing out past the Gooseberry
Rocks. It's lumpy. There are not so much waves as little hills and
hollows.

Now, in the southwest corner of Buzzards Bay, our choice is to
keep going or to cross the Bay and sleep at Cuttyhunk. I decide to
go for it and grab something to eat. While eating at the helm I mess
up a tack and swing the boat from a 30-plus-degree heel in one direction to a heel at least as steep in the other. This brings a yell from
below as Nancy lands on the floor.

"Sorry! I should have warned you!"

By 9:00 it is getting dark. We are approaching New Bedford. I
watch the trawlers coming in through Quicks Hole and making for
the New Bedford Harbor channel. One has its huge drum of cable
lit up like a Christmas display with a circle of white lights. Completely in the dark now I am close-hauled and racing across the bay,
looking for the unlit buoy that marks the end of the reef off West Island. I have to get around it before I can turn and make for our
mooring.

It is a slow process. I am using the GPS, which I have mounted
in the cockpit, to guide us. The GPS display will only stay lit for
about a minute after I hit the *light* button. It is not quite enough
time for me to get our coordinates and plot them on the large-scale
chart, the 1:20,000 "New Bedford and Approaches" chart I am
holding down with one hand in the windy cockpit. At about 10:00
Nancy pops up on deck to tell me she is going to bed. "Okay. See
you in the morning," I say, as I push *light* again.

The water is rushing past the boat like a vast pool of black ink,
with a sparkle of starlight dappling the wave tops. Low clouds lit and
colored by the lights of New Bedford are scudding by overhead.
Where we are headed it is all black. There are no lights on this end
of West Island, but the wind is becoming softer and warm. Using
the GPS and my thumb to measure our position on the chart, I see
we will finally pass 0.4 mile inside the buoy, where there is still
enough water to get through without running aground. I decide to
hold this course, but as we approach the reef, the sounder shows the

water depth dropping, until at 5 feet I change course. There is not supposed to be water that shallow out here.

LONDON turns gently out and the depth increases: 6, 9, 10, 12, 15. I tack again and we slip over the reef. I let her glide out into deeper water, relaxed now, with a gentle wind behind us, stretched out in the cockpit watching the clouds racing across the starlit heavens, water lapping along the hull. I am completely at peace. Later I take the chart below to see what went wrong with my navigation. In the lit cabin I can see that the unit on the chart I thought was a mile measure was in fact a half mile, and as a result my position estimate was far enough off to send us over a spot marked 2 feet at low water. I guess I should have been wearing my glasses. It was a grounding, like a rendezvous, just missed.

11

Sailing with the
Dictionary of Allusions

I begin to sweat as soon as I get out of the car. The sun is high, the marina office bright in the sun. I go inside looking for Dave. I need two blocks of ice and some diesel for the spare can.

"Maine, eh?"

"Can I owe you for the ice and the fuel?"

"I'll give you a slip."

Dave shows me where to park my old van for the next two or three weeks. Crushed clam shells crunch underfoot. I walk back to the office to leave him the keys. A car whizzes across the causeway and for a moment the red flag that reads "Live Lobsters" flutters in the breeze before again hanging limp. The car vanishes in the distance. Quiet returns.

Out on the boat I take off all my clothes and put on a pair of nylon shorts, boat sandals, and a hat. The two blocks of ice go in the cooler. I stow all the clothing, food, and gear I have brought. As usual there is too much stuff, but I always think, "What if I want to take a picture at night?" In goes the tripod. "What if I want to write?" In goes the laptop, and on and on, until I can barely fit it all in the dinghy.

By lunch I leave the mooring and sail northeast up the bay, past the entrance to Mattapoisett Harbor, toward the Cape Cod Canal. Passing through the canal I watch schools of bluefish drive smaller fish to the surface.

The wind is gentle and the sun halfway to the horizon when I come out the other end of the canal and float onto Cape Cod Bay. I point the bow at the open water midway between Provincetown and Plymouth, cook myself a hot meal on the stove below, and eat it in the cockpit.

I decide to stay out all night. The weather is fine. There will be a moon. Yesterday I drove 300 miles home from a business trip. Tonight I will drift.

The reading light over my bunk casts a soft light, more yellow than white, on the pages of my book. It is my first night at sea, after midnight, and I am alone.

I have the sails tied back in a configuration known as *heaving-to*. This keeps my boat stable and moving ahead dead slow. I backed the jib and tied the tiller with a line to one side of the cockpit, wrapping it tightly. It won't bang tonight, even in the slight roll of this gentle sea 10 miles off the Massachusetts coast. I pull a blanket over my legs and lie back to take a deep breath of warm salty air. I am in heaven. Or near enough.

I scan the list of allusions in the dictionary I am reading, looking for meaning, something with which to embellish the day. I bought this book, *The Oxford Dictionary of Allusions*, after seeing a review of it earlier in the summer. I first noticed the picture of the dictionary's cover centered at the top of the magazine page, in warm red and yellow tones, showing Narcissus gazing at his own reflection in the water.

I intend to color my sailing log with images and references from mythology, the classics, the fables. Through allusion I want to cast myself into an earlier reality, a past filled less with reason than personified mystery, and to enhance somehow that sense of adventure I seek at the end of the summer when I escape for a week or two in my little sailboat and poke my way up to Maine.

People ask if I get lonely. Yes, I do. I miss my family. I miss my friends. But sometimes it is good to be alone. The first day is always the most difficult, the next easier, the day after that more so. It takes a few days to accept the rhythm of the simple life, of just moving a boat up the coast. And it takes a few days to trust my boat again, to relax and to sleep—to lie on the bunk with the thin, hard mattress and know that the deep dark sea which lies just on the other side of the thin fiberglass hull, perhaps now 18 inches beneath my pillow, will not invade my warm and comfortable cabin and chill my dreams with her salty, suffocating, fish-rot breath. I pull up the quilt and settle deeper into my bunk.

I hear a low rumble. It gets louder. I swing out of the bunk, slip on my boat shoes, and climb up the companionway ladder into the open cockpit. What a night! The moon is out and the ocean is like a giant pane of undulating black glass. Stars sparkle and slip across the rolling ocean surface. A few light gray clouds drift across the dark sky. We are almost stationary in the water.

A cruise ship is bearing down on me. She seems to have every possible light on. The glow begins to illuminate the sea around me. The darkness fades like the flight of Erebus[10].

"How did she get so close?"

There is no one to answer me. I lunge for the engine starter. It starts with a cough and I push it into gear. The boat surges forward. I have forgotten that I lashed the tiller to one side. We make a circle. I bang my shins against something in the cockpit before getting the tiller untied to steer away from the ship's path. I haven't seen so much as a rowboat for the past five hours and now this. A ship!

Silhouettes of figures high up on her bridge look down on me as she steams past, a huge ornate mass of blazing light. I turn my boat to pass beneath her stern, read her name, and know what I should have guessed. She is THE REGAL PRINCESS. That's twice this month I have been under her bows.

Buzzards Bay was named, I suppose, for the ospreys floating high overhead on a fresh afternoon breeze. I imagine their view of the choppy water sparkling with whitecaps: a funnel-shaped bay separating the southern part of the Cape Cod landmass from the Massachusetts mainland. The bay is perfectly shaped to focus the wind down its tapered length to the spot where they dug the Cape Cod Canal.

A few weeks ago I sailed across the bay to pick up my friend Bruce, his kids, and their friends in the tiny harbor of Quissett. There had been a thick fog in the morning, but it burned off before lunch. We sailed out into the bay going nowhere and later returned to anchor in the harbor. Katherine showed off her new sunglasses while her younger brother chewed his sandwich. After lunch, the kids, Bruce, and I jumped off the side of the boat into the water, climbed out, and did it again. It was late in the afternoon by the time I left them on the town wharf. I went back out to the boat and wiped down the cabin sole from one end to the other. It had been covered in little sandy wet footprints. Then I rinsed the cockpit with a few buckets of salt water and set off for the quick sail back to my mooring in Fairhaven. Once I was outside the harbor jetty the breeze came up quickly. I was hauling for home at 5.5 and 6 knots. Streaks of fog reached down the bay on the increasing wind.

At first I wasn't worried. These are my home waters. I have marks, coordinates saved in the GPS, so that I can find my way home even in total oblivion. I turned on the GPS and steered for the first of these waypoints, the one I have named West 3, a point lying in open water halfway between West Island and Cormorant Rock. The GPS's tiny electronic screen displayed a small arrow pointing to West 3. The fog grew thicker. I could no longer see land on either shore.

After changing course to follow the GPS heading, I heard the first blasts of a ship's horn somewhere to my south. She blew loud. She blew deep. She blew five times.

Five blasts means, "You are standing into danger." Or put another way, "I am about to run you down."

Even so, there were two things I did not know. I did not know whether those blasts were directed at me or some other boat. And I did not know where the ship making the blasts was.

I could see a couple hundred yards upwind to where the sheet of gray fog, the leading edge of the approaching fog bank, hung dripping a foot or so above the rough, dark waves like a curtain drawn closed. Somewhere in that fog bank I guessed was a ship.

I set the auto-tiller and went below to scan the radio and hail the ship with a *Sécurité* call, but I had to rush back up to the cockpit after the boat heeled way over and I landed in the bunk. I struggled to get her back on course. My auto-tiller could not hold the boat on its upwind course in these conditions and I did not want to give way to leeward. I could make Nasketucket Bay on this tack.

The wind grew and the fog thickened. Alone in my island of visibility, every few minutes I heard the booming series of blasts from the thickest part of the approaching bank. There was only crackling and hiss from the radio below—any sense, any meaning, was swept away by the wind.

Finally, a hundred yards ahead, appeared the bow of a ship moving dead slow. I swung my boat around to run parallel past her chugging length and then turned again to pass under her stern. THE REGAL PRINCESS, a huge rumbling mass of steel, with a single blue-striped funnel, was there and then just as quickly gone, vanishing into the murk to the northeast. Once she passed me it was quiet, except for the whistling wind and the rush of the sea.

That was only three weeks ago. I just passed under her stern again. I think the Fates laugh at me in the night. My log entry for that night:

August 29, 2001
Liner passes. Again.
    Nearly 1 A.M. when she is well past. Set up heave-to and go below to get back in bunk. Lights out. Half an hour later. Before sleep, bang on deck. Go up to find a fresh new NE breeze. Wind goes from 0 to 17 in ten minutes. Soon am racing along through dark. After an hour wind settles down to a steady 14 knots and I get the auto-tiller set up. Eat some fruit and with more clothes on stretch out on deck. Later I wrap up in a quilt and watch the stars. Doze off, wake up with a start near Boston ship chan-

nel. Light in east already. Moon gone. Stars out. Wonder of light and
dawn. Erebus flees for the final time tonight.

On the last day of August I am moored in Portsmouth, New Hampshire in Back Channel, right behind the U.S. Navy yard. Navy police idle by in powerboats. There are taps at sunset.

It is a quiet, protected spot. A stormy night is forecast. I walk the few miles into Kittery Point to get groceries, my first steps this year in Maine. It is warm and close all night until the line of thunderstorms finally comes through before dawn, making the morning gray and murky. Rainwater from the night's deluge pours off the sails when I hoist.

I cruise down the Piscataqua River, round the point, and turn northeast. At first the wind is fitful; I race along and then glide into a dead calm. Late in the afternoon the breeze freshens out of the northwest until, as the sun is getting low in the sky, I am struggling to get onto a tack that will take me inside Wood Island to the anchorage just below Biddeford Pool.

Repeated calls to the Biddeford Pool Yacht Club on the radio and the cell phone have been met with silence. I decide to anchor if I can't get a mooring. I use the engine and sails to splash upwind through the chop and make my way finally between Wood and Gooseberry Islands.

Droplets splashed off the bow hang suspended for a moment as if confused before being grabbed by the wind and hurled horizontally across the deck. The spray is golden in the light of the setting sun, while the surface of the sea around me is a deep, dark blue. I am wet. I am cold. The sun and wind are in my face. I am having the best time. In some strange way I feel completely energized, almost invincible.

The anchorage is crowded. I am the last skipper to pull in. After puttering up and down rows of anchored boats, watching my depth meter and the sunset and studying the chart, I settle for a spot where the depth of the water under my keel is marginal, even with my

4-foot draft. The tide is 9 feet here tonight, and low water comes at 5:00 A.M. I set my alarm for 3:30 A.M. to check the depth an hour and a half before low.

Dark comes suddenly. The wind howls and the temperature drops. It is cold. The wind whips the tops off the little choppy waves. On deck I straighten a few lines, check the depth meter, and go below.

It is good to be in harbor. It is good to be below with the little alcohol stove on and the hatches mostly shut, eating a hot meal under a quilt. I fall asleep early. I sleep without dreams. When the alarm wakes me I can feel that the boat has pulled the anchor line taut in the strong current of the ebb. It is very dark. There is still plenty of wind, but nothing like before.

After twelve years of careful cruising, I am ready. This morning I will finally join that most exalted club of keel scrapers. I knew my time, my initiation, would come. It comes to us all. An unexpected grinding sound, a sudden lift, and you are in the club.

There are only three kinds of skippers: Those who have run aground, those who will run aground, and those that have but won't admit it.

Sailing books and magazines are filled with information on how to get afloat *after* you have run aground, but I found a remarkable absence of literature on just how to drive your keel into something solid in the first place. Having now planted my keel firmly on a rocky ledge, I feel ready to share my insights.

While you may have your own special way of touching bottom, a manner of which you are particularly proud, what I am about to describe is a proven method, one that may help you get your hull up out of the water and onto that tempting shoal or ledge. Running aground can be a fairly long and difficult process. While sailing we are concerned with staying afloat, much as we are with the set of our sails. Both maximize boat speed. Dragging the keel across a hard surface has been shown to slow down the boat. It is something I was taught to avoid.

Underway, I try to keep a sharp eye on the depth meter, constantly cross-check my position with landmarks and reference buoys, and update my position on the chart at regular intervals. If you do all this, it can be fairly difficult, if not impossible, to run your boat aground. So what to do?

First, *put yourself under some stress.* It prepares you for making those final critical mistakes. You can build up that tension by pushing for a destination just at the limits of your range and energy, by being out in weather beyond your comfort level, or by carefully keeping your equipment poorly maintained. You will probably find that once you manage to get a few threads of tension going, others will arise as if of their own accord. Stress begets more stress.

When I dropped the anchor, I knew I would need to wake up during the night to check the depth of water under my keel. I am up nearly two hours before low tide. I stumble up onto the cold, dark deck and watch the electric red numbers of the depth finder. The digital display starts out at 5.6 feet but descends to 3.9 as beneath my bare shivering feet LONDON's hull swings slowly across the dark water in the tidal current. There is no time to be lost; there are rocks down there. I haul up the anchor, being careful not to drop the wet chain on my bare toes. The engine starts right up and I putt past the sleeping boats out into the harbor channel. It is so early. I try not to wake anyone else.

This brings us to another good way to get your boat roughly ashore. *Sail in limited visibility.* Dark and fog, or even better, both dark and fog, really improve your odds. And once you get underway in the dark or fog, don't worry. Be confident. You know what you are doing. You know where you are! I can't emphasize this enough. It is the critical belief. Let me repeat, *You know where you are.* It can be hard to read charts in the dark breezy cockpit. Don't bother. You have been through here before. It's fine.

I dimly watch a nun pass some distance to my starboard while I am heading for the lighthouse and out to sea. This does not bother me. I know where I am.

Do it at speed. Get the boat moving. I set all my sails full in a good breeze. All the running lights are on. I race along entranced by the beauty of the phosphorescent wake. I stand and watch my wake, almost mesmerized by it. Looking astern helps.

Finally, it is important to drive on. All situations—ledges, bars, and shoals—are different, but often the best thing you can do to make it a really solid landing is nothing. In my case, as the boat lurches and then begins to lift, I stand still in the cockpit, mouth agape, as the sails and wind pull the boat up higher onto the ledge. The rule here is, *As you run aground, take no further action which might impede the grounding.*

I experience a powerful sensation of wonder as the boat rises up out of the water and grinds to a stop. I have achieved the nearly impossible—driven my boat ashore while surrounded by modern navigation aids, charts, a couple of GPSs, and at least one compass. I am filled with feelings of disbelief and pride. I have attained a sailing milestone. I could almost grab the boathook and pat myself on the back. I am in the club.

What sirens lured me onto these rocks? Who sang that sweet song? The lovely melody of my own incompetence. I think about what I have done. My boat is up on Wood Island's rocky Negro Ledge.

I check below. The bilge is still dry. I try leaning out over the water on the lee shrouds. Nothing shifts. I am like Andromeda chained to her rock.

I turn on the deck lights and pace around the shores of my new island. To project myself somewhere else, I imagine how this looks from shore: a cone of white light shining down from high on a tilted mast onto a white deck askew, in the distance the lighthouse on the rocky island, and beyond that just the dimmest glow of deep blue above the dark line of the ocean horizon.

At first I think the first two lobster boats out of Biddeford Pool will pass me by on their way to work, but the smaller, trailing boat turns toward me and the leader follows. I stand on the lazarette cover holding the backstay as the men, lit only by the green light of the electronics in their dark cabins, chug closer to me. The larger boat gingerly pokes her bow in toward the ledge LONDON is resting on.

A tall, thin man makes his way up onto the foredeck and yells across, "Is there any damage to the boat?"

"No. She seems okay."

"That's good. Freddie's got a smaller boat. He'll get right in there and pull you out. Get your line ready."

With that he backs off and the lobster boats bump and parley. Through the lit portholes of the second boat I can see someone rummaging below for rope. I quickly do the same and fasten it to my stern cleat.

"Good morning sir," says Freddie from the smaller boat as she pulls up near my stern.

"Toss me your line."

He looks me over.

"I'd prefer it fastened to the bow, sir."

I move my end of the line to the bow cleat.

"I'll spin her round and out of there. You lean her over as far as she'll go. Get her right over."

And spin me out he does. As the boat begins to move I can feel her sliding on the rock below. The tiller lurches as we begin the grinding spin. I wince and am afloat, free in the dark water, surfing at the end of a long tether through the dark morning, diesel exhaust in the air, feeling the full power of a lobster boat at work. Below again, I find no water in the deep bilge, and then I am up on deck smiling at Freddie and thanking him.

"I hope the rest of the day goes better than this."

"You'll be okay," he laughs. "The channel is over there."

The lobster boats are both gone as quickly as they had arrived.

I get my boat underway and creep out past the lighthouse, double-checking everything there is to check. It occurs to me that my attitude toward sailing and especially toward lobstermen is forever, and I do mean forever, changed.

A bit later, with Richmond Island nearly abeam and Cape

Elizabeth a bit further off, when I am confident I am surrounded by very deep water, I set up the auto-tiller and go below for a bowl of cereal and get the kettle going for a hot cup of tea. While waiting for the water to boil I look again into the deep, dark bilge. It is still dry. The day is beginning to get warm. Through the companionway I see some pilot whales pass astern. Another beautiful day in Maine.

August 31, 2001
At 4:00 A.M. get a depth reading of 3.9. Try shorten scope. Still too shallow. Dark anchor up and then engine on. Sails up in channel. Miss nun No. 6 in dark and run aground on SW ledge of Negro Island. Two lobster boats arrive. Smaller one, SEEKER, pulls me off. No leaks or apparent damage.

On to Portland. Breakfast and wash up underway. Arrive at Portland Yacht Services marina at 11:00 A.M. Afternoon with Nancy in Portland.

Stay over on mooring in Portland. Visit Greenpeace's RAINBOW EXPLORER in harbor. Bad night with annoying tangled mooring ball banging hull.

I have heard that Boothbay Harbor is a busy place and until now have avoided it, but since I can't make Robinhood Cove I decide to try Boothbay for the night. It is late Monday and the very end of Labor Day weekend. I pull into a harbor everyone else seems to have just left. Over the radio I am guided to a mooring in front of one of the seafood-restaurant-hotels. No one seems to want to collect a fee. I enjoy a fish dinner ashore and settle down in the cockpit to watch the ospreys diving for fish around the boat. One flies over my boat with a fish flapping in its claws. A few drops of salt water fall on me off the wet bird as it heads for the branches of a nearby spruce. Is this some lost Arcadia, disguised now as a tourist town? I decide to stay over.

There is another reason to linger. I think I am being poisoned. It is either the water from my boat's freshwater tank or the pot I am cooking in each night. After a series of timed experiments on my digestive system, I decide the problem is the thirty-plus-year-old aluminum pot. I buy a new one ashore and that will be the end of my problems.

It is a good day—an off day—showering, washing, and writing on my laptop. The tourist schooners and ferries slip through the water a few feet from my hull. A local church plays tunes over the harbor at sunset. I'll leave in the morning for the cruise up to Mt. Desert Island. I am beginning to doubt I will make it to Canada.

September 3, 2001, Labor Day
Motor most of the way to Halfway Rock. No wind and large swell from SW. Pilot whales. Lighthouses. Long line of sailboats inside heading S. I go outside Seguin Island in quiet weather. On other side sea builds with wind till approach to mouth of Sheepscot River has large trailing breaking sea. After jibe, furl in jib and on main alone make Boothbay.

September 4, 2001
$25.80 groceries, $1.00 paper, $1.50 ice, $5.00 breakfast
Boothbay stay-over. Approaching cold front.
Buy new pot $24.00 and supper $18.00

I make it to Northeast Harbor on Mt. Desert Island three days later.

The first day out of Boothbay I have a quick and wild sail. My reef blows out crossing the mouth of the St. John's River and I struggle to keep the boat stable while I get things tied down again. On the stretch to Tenants Harbor I sail in as much wind as I've ever sailed in, but once I get the sails set correctly LONDON performs beautifully—sailing right into the wind with a steady swaying effort. The wind screeches across my ears and for a time, before I make the sudden warm quiet of Tenants Harbor, I imagine I can hear a swarm of Furies in the whistling air bent on vengeance somewhere downwind.

The next day is completely different. Calm and cool, just enough breeze to keep moving along. I am cutting out of Muscle Ridge

Channel for Penobscot Bay when a bat lands on my sail. I let it rest there undisturbed. Pilot whales swim by. An eagle watches me swing by the southern tip of Vinalhaven from its perch on a golden slab of granite. The pines make a broad and dark green line above the stone.

A few days later in Northeast Harbor I decide to explore the famous carriage roads ashore. I walk into the village and stop at the bike shop I spotted on a grocery and ice run. Inside I meet Steve, the proprietor. We swap sailing stories. Misadventure at Biddeford Pool is still on my mind. He tells me about his 26-foot Tanzer dragging in a gale on Somes Sound and how he managed to get her off the rocks. Then I get on a mountain bike and pedal up a long hill, past an old stone gatehouse, and into the park. The air is warm and humid. I am soon riding shirtless through the woods.

I stop at Jordan Pond House for lunch. I devour a fresh salad and popovers and jam with many glasses of ice tea, a cornucopia after my plain boat fare. I listen to the voices around me. Yellow jackets buzz through the conversations to steal licks of butter and strawberry jam. Their tiny wings sparkle silver in the sun.

After lunch I pedal down a series of gravel carriage trails with only a vague idea where they are taking me. It is enough to be ashore and have the breeze cool my sweat. The trail gets steeper. I stop occasionally to walk my bike and then get on and pedal again. I ride over the top of a mountain and down the length of Somes Sound, a 5-mile fjord running up into the heart of the island. Late in the afternoon I make it back to the village and ease out of the bike seat. My legs feel numb and feeble. I shower, have a beer, and nap till supper. After supper I fall asleep listening to the Canadian maritime forecast from across the Bay of Fundy. I have seen the fog sitting out there on the cold water a mile or two out. I am not going out there in that fog.

On September 9 I make my way to Tom Cod Cove, just south of Castine near the Holbrook Island Sanctuary. Here I find a colony of seals, ospreys, and even bald eagles that I will watch for the next two days. On the way here I sailed the length of Eggemoggin Reach, the sailing equivalent of a full dress Sunday promenade down the boulevard. Unfortunately I forget that my damp underwear is strung out to dry on the forward lifelines, somewhat spoiling the dignified appearance of my little sloop.

I have been musing on a memory long forgotten. I sailed down this same stretch of silver water with my parents many years ago on a boat that I think was called an Isleboro 17.

September 10, 2001

Wake to foggy situation. After visiting seals in dinghy to photo them, go out anyway and after not being able to see the Cape, decide to go to Castine for supplies and diesel. Spend $5.00 diesel and $11.00 on groceries.

Land at Castine town dock. Photograph boat from above. Day looking better. Out again into Penobscot Bay. Once out I am facing a wall of fog. No Islesboro, racing scudding clouds, and wind and chop in face. Retreat to Holbrook Island Sanctuary and anchor off beach. Meet a woman sailing along in a small catboat who is struggling to get her second reef in. I offer assistance and we chat for a while. She is from upriver. I go ashore and wander around park but am driven back to breezy beach by vicious mosquitoes. Get half in water. Wind comes up so much I decide to move boat back to Tom Cod Cove. Although I am in sun all day, a wall of fog is racing by offshore and sweeping over parts of Castine I can see.

A good day among the Islands of the Blest[11].

The morning of September 11 is clear and pleasant. The fog blew off during the night in a cool, fresh breeze that whistled in the rigging till after 2:00 A.M. A hurricane is passing 300 miles offshore. The marine forecast predicts large swells from the storm. I am up and on my way at first light. I will sail southwest across Penobscot Bay and then again stop at Tenants Harbor. I have trouble all day with the cell phone and have been unable to reach Nancy. Late in the day I walk up to a phone booth in front of a convenience store at Tenants Harbor. It is about 5:30 in the evening.

Nancy tells me about the World Trade Center towers falling down, the hijacked jets, the Pentagon, the terror, the bravery, the chaos—our daughter in D.C. and our nephew and brother-in-law in New York City are all safe. I look around outside. A pickup pulls up in a spray of gravel. The sun shines. On the main road cars whine past the white clapboard houses. Everything seems normal. I wonder if Nancy got it right. I go back into the store. There is no TV. Back at the dock I talk to the proprietor about the terrorists. I need to hear it from someone else. I say something like, "We've got to go over there and destroy those terrorist camps."

The woman lifts her head from the ledger of accounts she has spread out across the picnic table. She looks me in the eye and sighs.

"How you going to do that?"

I go out on the boat, dig out my Walkman radio, and go up on deck. I sit in the cockpit with my mouth open and listen to the news. It is horrible. I talk to Nancy again and promise to hurry home.

On the morning of September 12 I leave Tenants Harbor very early. There are still big swells, so I head straight out to sea, outside all the little ledges and islands, to where the water is deeper and the sea is more settled. I try several times to call Kate, our daughter who lives in D.C., on my cell phone, but I cannot get through. I do hear later from Nancy that Kate is safe and with her friends.

Once past Seguin Island, I turn toward the coast and pull in at Pott's Harbor in Casco Bay for the evening. I quickly anchor outside the mooring area and go ashore to eat at the Dolphin Restaurant. It is here that I see the first image of the disasters on the cover of a local newspaper—a cascade of fire down a skyscraper face. I have been listening to the news on my Walkman radio all day while sailing. I have talked on the phone with friends in Boston.

It has been an empty day on the water. The lobstermen are staying in port; there are no planes to fly the catch, and the lobster pens are nearly full. I will see one or two boats all day. There are no planes overhead. No jet trails. It is unnaturally quiet.

I am completely deflated by events. The Philistines are among us. All illusion is shattered. My trip is over. I get on the phone and arrange to have the boat hauled for the winter in Portland, at the yard where I stopped on the way north. I rent a car and drive home.

12

Winter 2001–2002

Portland Yacht Services haul out LONDON with her mast still up and put her on the edge of the boatyard near the narrow-gauge railway line. From her cockpit, now some 8 feet above the solid earth, I can watch the boat traffic in the Portland Harbor entrance until my reverie is broken by the steam whistle of the little train rattling by in the foreground, carrying kids huddled in brightly colored parkas around the edge of the harbor. An engineer dressed in the traditional railroad overalls waves a dirty leather glove out the window of the small, black steam engine. The dust from their passage settles on LONDON's white decks.

Other than the rattle of trains, the winter passes quietly for LONDON. The only job I take on is the repair of a broken bronze cockpit locker hinge. The hinge pin froze in place and snapped. I remove the hinge from the boat and try to buy a new one from a supplier that still makes Cape Dory parts, but after I place my order I get a message on my answering machine that their forge is broken. The only choice seems to be to find a machinist who can remove the bronze pin from the hinge and replace it with a new one.

One day in January while walking from my office into the village for lunch, I notice a low white building set back from the street with a single word, *Acadian*, over its door. I remember once seeing a flatbed truck parked in front of this building loaded with metal stock.

The next day I walk up to the building, look closely at the word overhead, and push the wooden door open. I find myself in a dimly lit office. Behind a desk mostly hidden under pieces of paper a man is eating a sandwich. He turns to look up at me. An open door on the side of the office leads into a shop. I see machine tools.

"Is this a machine shop?"

My question hangs in the air by the sheer lightness of its stupidity.

He agrees to fix the hinge for me. I leave the pieces with him and he scrawls my phone number on a scrap of paper. It goes onto the pile of paper as I go out the door.

Over the course of the winter I stop by every few weeks to see how the hinge is progressing. I come to enjoy my talks with my new friend, who turns out to be a young eighty years old. He mostly works alone, although I sometime see his wife there during the day. He tells me her attention and care are responsible for his good health and happiness.

The shop contains about sixty pieces of machining equipment. I am not sure which one he uses on my hinge, but when I do get it back from him, with a new stainless steel pin, it swings better than ever. He says he had built a similar hinge for someone's knee. I pay him $15.

I know that, as soon as LONDON is launched in the spring, I will immediately be off on a three- or four-day sail home. While she is still on land I make lists and get her stocked with food and water.

I put the batteries back in the boat and test them with the voltmeter. I test the auto-tiller and radio. I ask the boatyard to work on the engine, and they replace an oil seal, the impeller, the zinc anode, and belts and filters. I replace the water filter I installed three years before during LONDON's restoration with a brand-new one and load aboard the sails, sleeping bags, and other gear I have taken home.

I hate to admit it now, but I had LONDON on the market through the winter. The boat broker called me when people showed interest, and they came to look her over. I had the idea that I would sell LONDON and buy a bigger Cape Dory, one on which I could take out more people for longer trips. There would be more privacy. Several people told me I was crazy to sell her after putting so much work and money into her. I received several e-mails asking why I wanted to sell such a fine boat. I blithely explained how much I enjoyed the restoration work and that I would gladly take on a similar project again.

As the winter wore on, so did the recession. Spending more money on a new boat, however great a deal it might be, seemed less and less realistic, but I stubbornly kept her for sale, even though I had a growing sense of how comfortable I had become with LONDON. I looked at other boats and wondered what it would take to become comfortable with them. It seemed a lot.

Slowly I began to ask myself if I really needed another boat. LONDON really is the perfect size for me to sail alone or with a few friends. With her 4-foot draft I can go lots of places others cannot, including up on that ledge at Wood Island. I did get off again.

About a week before her planned launch I take her off the market and heave a private sigh of relief. I still have LONDON. I hope I have not insulted our relationship by attempting to sell her. When I look back at this period I can no longer imagine what I was thinking. Any separation from LONDON now seems very foreign. It was something I had to try, something she and I had to go through, almost like the stupid affair some people need to have at the end of the beginning of their marriages.

All that is behind us now; I hope she has forgiven me. I think she has, but if there is some price to pay, I will pay it. It is only right.

The weather is again getting warm. I focus on my plan to sail her home. The first part of my route from Portland, Maine to Fairhaven, Massachusetts is across a fairly exposed stretch of water. I want the weather to be good for a few days before setting off. My friend Gary comes to Maine one day in late May to help me get underway. We get to the boatyard, climb into the boat, and turn on the weather radio for one last check. A gale is forecast for the weekend. I walk into the office and postpone my launch.

Gary and I install the repaired hinge, scrub LONDON, and spend most of the day hanging around in Portland. We have fish and chips at a wharf restaurant. We feed the stray cats.

A few days later, on the Saturday afternoon when I would have been sailing, I log onto the Internet and check the conditions out at sea as reported by a buoy in the Gulf of Maine. There is rain, lots of wind, and 10-foot seas. I am happy to be ashore. LONDON waits in the wet, her covers off, nursing perhaps, even now, a small grudge.

13

Two Returns with Rich

*Many things are cured by wind and sea, if you stay on deck
with them long enough.*

—Bernard Moitessier

My friend Rich came sailing with me twice during the 2002 summer
season. Our first sail began in Portland, Maine on the morning of
the summer solstice, the longest day of the year.

Nancy, Rich, and I arrive at the boatyard in Portland early. The
yard is making the most of the light and the good weather. As we
get out of the car I see LONDON is already in the water, tied to a
mooring. The launch driver takes Rich and me out to her. When we
step aboard she rocks a bit and then stabilizes. It is good to feel her
move. I check the bilge. It is dry. We start "Old Reliable" and motor
to the big floating dock they call the waterfront to tie up.

We load LONDON with the last of the gear, bend on the sails, blow
up the inflatable, and mount its outboard. When we are done Rich
and I will leave for Fairhaven. LONDON is going home.

The waterfront is exposed to the harbor. As ships go in and out of
Portland their wakes rock the floating docks. As each wave passes us
on its inevitable way to shore, we watch the dock sections lift and roll
along their length. The swaying makes Nancy feel sick. She leaves
to get us some coffee and bagels. I am on the foredeck fiddling with
the jib halyards. Sweat runs down my back. A small spot on the

index finger of my left hand is sore; I banged an old splinter scab last night while loading the car. Nancy returns and the three of us sit together on the floats, ride up and down on the harbor wakes, drink coffee, and try to cool off.

After the break, it is time to say goodbye to Nancy. She will drive the car back to Massachusetts. I take LONDON's tiller as Rich pushes her away from the dock. He hops on board amidships. We swing away from the dock and start toward the harbor channel.

I have put the working jib on the roller-furler and left the genoa below. There are small craft warnings up. I pinch my sore finger again while adjusting the jib sheets. There is some pus under the skin. I pick at it—it won't drain.

We follow the channel out of the harbor past Portland Head Light and head southeast. The wind is from the southwest. We get the main and jib hoisted but leave the motor on to help push the boat into the chop and keep us pointing higher into the wind. Water is soon flying across the foredeck and sometimes streaming over the cabintop and dribbling into the cockpit.

By the time we get clear of the land the temperature has dropped about 40 degrees. We put on more clothing. The boat makes about 5 knots. It is 10 A.M. and I am feeling seasick. I never feel seasick. Ever. My finger begins to throb. The boat lurches. I keep banging the finger trying to hang on. Rich sticks his head up through the companionway. He looks tired. Earlier he said he didn't get enough sleep last night.

"Let's get the auto-tiller set up," he says. "Where is it?"

"In the port berth side locker."

He brings it up on deck. I plug *auto* in and press the button to move the mechanical arm. Nothing happens. I fiddle with the wires, pull the arm, test the connection. Nothing. I cannot believe this. I tested the *auto* a week ago. I go below and lift the cushion to get into the under-berth locker where the manuals are kept. I hold the cushion up with my head, brace against the hull with one hand so I won't fall across the heaving boat, and leaf through the locker with the other hand. I find the manual and sit down heavily as the boat drops into a trough. I find my glasses and the phone number of the service department and catch my cell phone as its slides across the table. I call the manufacturer's service line in New Hampshire. Incredibly, in a few minutes I am speaking to an expert on *auto*. This is wonderful. Things have changed so fast, even in sailing, with cell phones and the Internet. Information is everywhere.

I go up on deck to get a better phone signal, but with the wind in my ears it is hard to hear the man on the phone. I come to understand that while there may be enough voltage to light *auto*'s compass display, the current may not be sufficient to drive the mechanical arm. I tell Rich what I have learned.

Rich gives me that look, the look that says something is broken on my boat. Again. It is nothing new to him. He was there for LONDON's first cruise, when "Old Reliable" died and he ended the afternoon spread-eagled across the bow trying to avert disaster as the boat sailed at the dock too fast. I hate that look. I know I checked this. It is so unfair. If we don't get this fixed we are going to be tiller slaves. We have a long way to go.

Rich and I begin to look for loose battery connections, but neither of us wants to spend much time upside down in the cockpit locker with the lid banging his head, his stomach surging as the boat rises and falls, lurches and rolls. My sore hand makes everything harder. We decide to steer by hand for a while. We will think about it. I take the tiller. Rich goes below for a nap.

While he is below, and I hope asleep, I discreetly and delicately throw up over the side. I immediately feel better and begin to eat a sandwich I brought for lunch. I sit in the cockpit in the breeze and the salty spray. The waves are steep, running 3 or 4 feet, breaking slightly. One in every twenty splashes over the bow; one in a hundred streams water across the cabintop. A gull dives down and soars aloft. A tug and barge appear astern from Portland and are soon past us on a more southerly course. At some point in mid-afternoon I see that the longitude on the GPS is now reading 69 degrees and some minutes. We are way out, further east than Cape Cod, almost to Platts Bank. I hear Rich getting up.

I make the first tack of the day. He pops up through the companionway. We are now on a heading for Portsmouth, New Hampshire. Rich looks a lot better.

When I am out on the ocean, surrounded only by water, the mountains of the nearest land a dim, featureless loom on the horizon, I feel I am in a kind of desert—an ocean desert—a landscape of endless water. It is easy to succumb to this emptiness, to the ambulatory pace, to the expansive sameness, to breathe a sigh of *ennui* and ask, Why am I here? Is it only to reef, to tack, to steer? Is this fun?

But like most sailors I know, I love studying charts and maps. Our chart reveals the form, features, and contours of the ocean bottom; it allows us to form a mental picture of the undersea landscape and fills the gaps in our senses. Rich and I are not in the middle of nowhere; we are approaching Platts Bank. The chart tells us where we are, how deep the water is, and illustrates with undulating light blue lines the gradations of the slopes beneath. The abbreviation *so M* is printed on the chart a little way back from where we now are. It means soft mud.

There must be something more down there, some 90 fathoms beneath our little boat. Ninety fathoms is deep. At about 6 feet to a fathom, that's 540 feet, or twenty of LONDON's boat lengths from the surface to the soft mud. I want to know more about what lies beneath us, to see below the surface, to know what we are passing over, to see the very bottom.

As part of a major study to explore the continental shelf, the Continental Margin Program, the U.S. Geological Survey and the Woods Hole Oceanographic Institution launched the deep submergence vehicle ALVIN to dive not far from this spot, on the slopes of Platts Bank itself. It was May of 1968; their mission was to photograph and examine the bottom[12]. The following is an excerpt from the dive log:

The dive commenced at 0905. Bottom was reached at 0935 in 100 meter depth. The bottom was fine sand and some silt, but showed no ripple marks. The bottom was underlain by hard rock at a depth of 6 to 8 inches. Numerous Cerianthus tubes, sponges, and some sea anemones but very few fish were observed. Only scattered cobbles or small boulders were seen. Proceeded up the southeast slope of Platts Bank which reached an inclination of about 12 degrees and encountered currents of about 0.8-1.0 knots from the North...

Cerianthus is a burrowing tube anemone. They look like miniature palm trees, together making a sparse forest across the bottom. The pale, waving fronds originating in the center remind me of a wet artichoke heart.

In 2002 Robert Buchsbaum published an article titled "Hiking to Georges Bank" in which he imagines a hike one might have taken across the Gulf of Maine thousands of years ago:

> In the time of the last continental glacier 11,000 years ago, when sea levels were about 300 feet lower than they are today, you could actually have hiked a "Gulf of Maine Trail" through heather-clad hills to Georges Bank and perhaps run into mammoths, mastodons, and musk oxen.
>
> This landscape now lies beneath the sea, and cod, hake, and flounder have replaced the mammoths. But what if you could, by some magical transformation, follow this Gulf of Maine Trail today? [13]

Back on the surface, although we aimed for Portsmouth, as the afternoon progressed we have slipped to the leeward. The sun is getting low in the sky as we pass to the north of Boon Island. It is clear we will need to tack out and then back in again to make it upwind and into Portsmouth Harbor. Rich thinks we should stay out all night.

"Why bother? We'll lose an hour getting in there and another getting out. Let's just keep going!"

I have had a nap and am feeling fresh. A good friend is urging me to sail on—to sail through the night of the summer solstice, with a full moon and a fresh breeze. There really is no decision to make.

"Ready about. Hard a lee!"

With that cry and the swing of the tiller, we are on our way back out to sea. We pass to the south of Boon Island. Looking at the chart, I see Boon Island is surrounded by a series of humps and rocky ledges. In the growing dark we concentrate on keeping well clear of the rocky reefs. Buchsbaum's description of a kelp-covered reef on the floor of the Gulf of Maine probably captures the murky landscape we are passing over.

> The kelp forms a dense canopy that floats back and forth at the whim of currents and waves that crash against the rocky shoreline. Cunner fish, tautogs, lobsters, rock crabs, brittle stars, and sponges find hiding places under the waving kelp blades, inside the nooks within the jumble of rocks, and in the rootlike holdfasts that cement the kelp to the rocks. Sea urchins, the wildebeests of this habitat, make open patches on the rocks by grazing on kelp and other seaweed. These "urchin barrens" are covered by colorful sea stars, sea anemones, sea squirts, and pink calcareous algae.

We watch in the failing light for the lights on the Isles of Shoals and, much later in the long night, for the lighthouses of Cape Ann, Massachusetts.

When cruising *by the book*, one of the first things to be established on a voyage is a watch schedule. Rich and I simply don't do that. We have known each other for twenty years, sailed together for much of that time, and can just work it out as it happens. We both know what needs to be done. Either of us can sleep easily with the other at the tiller. There is a kind of freedom in this ad hoc watch schedule. There are no alarms and rigid four hours on, fours hours off. We each get something closer to the natural cycles of sleep we need.

It is surprising how quickly we fall into this supportive routine and how well we sleep, even with the noisy one-cylinder diesel running as we beat into 25 knots of head-on wind. With the boat heeled over into hull-banging waves, we crawl one after another into the sleeping bag in the lee berth and in a few moments are asleep, only to wake to some unusual motion, some unusual noise. I will always remember the sleep I had on this voyage, however broken and disparate, as some of the sweetest sleep of my life. To be in that fat cotton sleeping bag, wedged behind the table on the low side of the sloped cabin, is a warm and religious experience. I sleep the sleep of the deep.

Once during the night, somewhere between the Isles of Shoals and Cape Ann, I am woken by banging overhead. Sounds like metal on fiberglass. I am damp with a cold sweat and chilly. At first I think it is just the jib sheet block rattling in the aluminum track overhead. The boat lurches and rolls. The diesel chugs in the dark. The noise seems to be coming from something hitting the cabintop. I pull myself out of the bag, don my fleece jacket, pull my slicker back on, and go up on deck to grunt at Rich, who seems frozen at the tiller, puffy-faced, fighting sleep. With the flashlight I see the aft lee inner shroud has come undone at the turnbuckle. The turnbuckle swings back and forth in an arc at the end of the shroud wire. It strikes the cabintop on every completed arc.

"Damn!"

There is beauty in the silvery arc made by the wire of the shroud swinging through the flashlight beam. Like the swing of the hypnotist's pendulum, it entrances us.

I flip on the deck lights and, wearing an inflatable life jacket with a built-in harness clipped to the jacklines we've rigged, I slide my butt forward over the cabintop to snatch the dangling inner shroud and pull it toward the flapping toggled screw fastening. Because I just woke up, because it is dark, because one of my hands is sore and inflamed, because we are still flying across the sea as we have been all day with the lee rail dipping into the ocean every ten waves, or because I am trying so very hard not to drop any of the little rigging bits into the dark ocean forever—for one or all of these reasons it takes a good fifteen minutes to get the turnbuckle fastened to the deck toggle. When I am finally done I slide back to the cockpit and relieve Rich so he can get some sleep. God knows how long he has been on deck.

My hand is hot and throbbing from the infection in my finger. I keep picking at it. It hurts too much to leave it alone. I feel as if I am being stung by a wasp, again and again. Finally I make a quick lurching trip through the dark cabin to the medicine cabinet. I swallow two or three Advil. In minutes the pain is gone. Only then can I give my finger a soak in some cold ocean water scooped into a tin cup, put on some antibiotic ointment and a clean cool bandage, and leave the finger alone.

For the rest of this voyage we live out scenes of isolated events, unaware of duration or even sequence. Some things remain clear.

At one point, when we are sailing near Stellwagen Bank, I stare off to port and, watching the sea with sleepy eyes, see a whale fin rise up on a course parallel to ours. The fin stays there cutting through the surface for a full two minutes before slipping below. It does not return. In "Hiking to Georges Bank," Buchsbaum describes the bottom here:

> After crossing the miry depth of Stellwagen Basin, you enter the Stellwagen Bank National Sanctuary and begin a climb up the 200-foot slope to the Stellwagen Bank. Boulders and cobbles left by the last glacier cover the slope here, providing habitat for lobsters, cod, and haddock. Where the cobble bottom has not been trawled, there is an abundant cover of sponges, hydroids, bryozoans, and tunicates, and many juvenile fish and shrimp. Near the top, depressions in the sand riffles created by a recent storm are covered with broken shells of ocean quahogs, providing another place for fish and invertebrates to hide.

Up on the surface, lost in a dreamy reverie of the deep, I turn around to see that the inflatable dinghy we were towing is gone. It is very early in the morning. I put the tiller between my knees, get the binoculars, and look down our wake. Maybe a mile and a half behind I can see a bump on the surface of the sea. It takes a good half

Pete and the Whale

hour to go back, pick it up, and head southwest once again. I go below as Rich takes the tiller. When he asks me if I am tired, I say no. I fall asleep instantly.

When I awake we have sailed into another world, a cloud world without feature. White air, glassy sea. We can see half a mile of the ocean's surface but there is no horizon, no sky, just a close, damp white warmth. It feels electric. The moving boat seems to leave a static trail in this atmosphere. We talk very little. It feels like we are floating through the heart of a developing thunderhead.

Our evening arrival at the Cape Cod Canal is timed just about right. We power against the last of the flood current and make a quick stop for fuel at the Sandwich harbor of refuge. The engine has been on since Portland, thirty-three hours, the longest "Old Reliable" has ever run by far. When we emerge from the other side of the canal it is dark. We use waypoints saved in my GPS to help us find our way to Bird Island, then to Mattapoisett's outer buoy, and finally to pass outside of Cormorant Rock before turning into Fairhaven and my mooring. We tie up to the mooring at about 10:00 P.M. after sailing for some thirty-six hours.

We go ashore the next morning. On Monday I see my doctor. He winces as I unwrap my finger.

"It's good you came in. You could lose your hand if that went untreated much longer. You need a hand surgeon."

He sends me back to the waiting room while he makes the arrangements. A hand surgeon? When I meet her, an hour later, she is equally reassuring.

"It's rare, but people can die from things like this. Have you been handling fish?"

She operates on my finger the next day. She is extremely strong and squeezes my numbed finger until I think she must have flattened it. The tiny piece of black wood she extracts is sent to the lab with other samples. I spend the next two weeks with my arm in a sling to keep my hand up at shoulder level. I eat large antibiotic pills, which make me sleepy. During this period I come home from work, have supper, and fall asleep at about 8:00 P.M. I get up twelve hours later and even though I am at home and comfortable—or as comfortable as you can be while sleeping with your hand elevated over your head—it is nothing like the peace I felt in that sleeping bag on the boat.

I remember a line from Rockwell Kent's book *N by E*, his account of a 1929 voyage to Greenland in the sloop DIRECTION: "My blankets are of magic stuff; drawing them over me I'm wrapped in sleep."

Shipwrecked on the Greenland coast, the artist was saved by Eskimos and transported to Denmark. He returned to New York City and continued to create the illustrations for *Moby Dick*. He knew about the deep sleep at sea.

When I tell my surgeon about the effects of the pills, she tells me I am depressed from the wound to my hand. I listen but know I am not depressed. I am drugged. When I finish taking the pills, my land sleep patterns return to normal.

It is more than ten days before I have enough dexterity to sail again. When I do go sailing, a sudden gust against the mainsail as I approach the harbor pinches my lazy fingers between the mainsheet and the hard arm of the teak tiller. The incision on my finger breaks open. Still, I am out on the water. The pain is soon gone.

The second return with Rich begins in Nantucket Harbor near the end of the summer. On the way out of the harbor, where we have spent a night tied to a mooring that cost the incredible sum of $55, we spot a Coast Guard inflatable out near First Point. A big yawl is up on the sand. We swing by to have a look. The sight brings back memories of LONDON's first trip to Nantucket. The owner is working near the keel with a shovel. I take some pictures with the long lenses. We turn again and head back out to sea. In this same spot years ago I saw other sailors dragging for their anchor, bobbing in a dinghy with a grappling hook, after their anchor line was cut by a passing mega-yacht. They too had drifted into these shallows.

As soon as we clear the ends of Nantucket's sunken harbor jetties we swing to the west. We will take a different route home, closer to the southern shoals and banks—right over the tops of some of them. It is a quiet day. The forecast is for the winds to be light and variable, less than 10 knots out of the southwest. Rich is happy to sit in the cockpit and keep watch. I stay below and read. Every thirty minutes I mark our progress on the chart as Rich reads me the position off the GPS mounted over the bridge deck. I study what is ahead on the chart and tell him how to adjust our heading to avoid the shallowest spots. It is a quiet, cloudless morning. We have all the sails up and amble along the northern shore of Nantucket at an average rate of about 3 knots.

We pass over Tuckernuck Shoal just to the north of a spot where a thumb of deep water cuts into the bold blue shape of the shoal on the chart. To the northeast and the southwest are shallow spots where at low water the depth is only 6 or even 2 feet deep. With the GPS and our regular plots, we are confident we know where we are to within about 30 feet. It is a calm day and an easy sail. We would not do this if it was blowing and the sea was up. We could find ourselves bouncing along the sandy bottom in the troughs.

We skim the northern edge of Edwards Shoal and then the Norton. After lunch I take the tiller. Rich has turned a lovely pink from the sun; he goes below. I try to eat lunch early while the boat is still level, before the afternoon southwest comes up. By 12:30 it starts to blow, and by the time we are off Cape Poge on Martha's Vineyard I put a reef in the main to lessen the weather helm, although I keep the big genoa all the way out. My can of seltzer slides across the fiberglass surface of the bridge deck and comes to rest upright against the lower side of the cockpit.

The tidal current is a big factor sailing in these waters. This morning the dying flood was pushing on our forward quarter as we moved along the northern shore of Nantucket. It flowed across our track as we passed across the middle of the gap between the Vineyard and Nantucket. By the time we near the Chops in the mid-afternoon it will swing in our favor, and the 2-plus knots of the new ebb current will help us tacking later this afternoon into the wind gusting up Vineyard Sound.

As we make our way across the wind shifts off the East and West Chops, we are set to the east and go across to Nobska Point on the Cape to make our big tack and begin the pursuit of a large, black wooden schooner tack for tack down Vineyard Sound. LONDON goes upwind best in a stronger breeze, and with the current in our favor, we begin to make real progress down the Sound. The wind blowing against the tide makes the Sound rolly and wet, but the water is warm. On one tack we look ahead at the high, firm hills of the Vineyard, and on the other we see the low pristine shapes of the sparsely populated Elizabeth Islands. It is a beautiful place to sail on an August afternoon.

These two geographic features, the west side of the Vineyard and the Elizabeth Islands, stand out on a map as almost parallel arcs. These arcs mark where the edge of a huge glacier stood still in the last stages of the Pleistocene Epoch. The western edge of the Vineyard was formed by a glacial standstill that seems to have lasted for 1,000 years; this was the southern extent of the ice sheet. Even though the glacier would reach no further south, it continued to act like a gigantic conveyor belt, carrying soil and rock in the ice that was still slipping up to its edge, breaking off, and melting on what is now the western side of Martha's Vineyard. This formation is known as a terminal moraine. Then, perhaps 13,000 years ago, the glacier suddenly retreated to where the Elizabeth Islands are today. This second standstill produced another pile of glacial debris, which would eventually become the Elizabeth Islands. The warming climate not only led to the retreat of the glaciers, but also to a rising sea level. As the sea rose it flooded in over the lowlands and caused the Vineyard and Nantucket to become islands. The filling of what is now Buzzards Bay by the waters of the Atlantic occurred about 5,000 or 6,000 years ago[14].

The black schooner[15] ahead makes her way into Tarpaulin Cove for the night. We consider following and anchoring there, but streams of high, thin clouds coming in from the west and a marine forecast of a strong front tomorrow spook me into keeping on for Fairhaven tonight. We take the reef out before we reach Quicks Hole. Once we pass through Quicks Hole and enter Buzzards Bay the weather becomes calm. I take advantage of the absence of boat motion to begin cooking a hot supper. I no sooner get the pot of lentil pilaf bubbling on the stove than the breeze associated with the approaching sky begins to blow and heel the boat.

"Just keep it level for a few more minutes!" I call out to Rich.

"I'm trying."

By the time we settle down to eat our bowls of steaming grain, we need to brace ourselves in the cockpit. A fork put down on the deck slides to the lowest point of the cockpit. We eat and do the dishes quickly. By sunset we are both up on deck.

The buoy off the tip of West Island is our first mark. We use the GPS to aim slightly to the starboard of it. By the time we pass the mark it is dark. Rich finds the buoy in the gloom with the beam of the handheld spotlight. Then we use the other pre-saved GPS waypoints to find our way down Nasketucket Bay and to slip up to my mooring in the dark.

After I pull the mooring lanyard through the bow chock and fasten it to the cleat, I stay out on the foredeck and look at the night. The forecast today was for light and variable winds, 10 knots southwest. We had everything from near calm to 20-plus knots. That is quite a range, but I guess you could say 10 knots was the median.

I look up to admire the luminous moon. Thin clouds seem to glow and swirl high overhead. The moon shining through the misty air reminds me of a favorite painting, which I saw on a visit to London a few years ago. Nancy and I were at the gallery in Somerset House. One picture, a Rubens, filled me with wonder. It hung as if almost forgotten on a small wall between a corner and a door. It looked, well, it looked like tonight: a luminous moon behind diffuse clouds, the colors of a marine night sky, with the stars, like the stars tonight, glowing through the gossamer strands of cloud. It was painted in 1637 and titled *Landscape by Moonlight*. I stood for a long time and took it in. It was somehow new and exciting, yet familiar. The museum guidebook says the artist achieved an effect of nocturnal solitude. The landscape is bathed in a bright moonlight with warm glowing colors. He used more light than is natural to create an illusion of perception[16].

That is the effect tonight. It seems there is more light than natural. The clouds and the water reflect what light there is, brightening the night and the sky. The painting showed a scene of the flat Dutch countryside with river water and a field. I am looking across a coastal marsh, low islands, and a mooring field. And yet the skies are so similar it is eerie.

I hear Rich come back up on deck and turn to look at him.

"Watching the moon?" he asks.

"Yup."

But it is more than that. I am thinking about the gap between the dabs of colored paint on a board—that painted image I so loved—and the real scene around me. About the gap between the maritime adventure read about or dreamed about during the safe winter months, when even an ocean crossing seems simple, and the real challenge of making a short trip in the face of racing gray clouds and the vagaries of weather, across expanses of water that always present at least a small adventure, however sheltered the bay or warm the water.

"Hey Rich."

"Yeah?"

"Thanks for the help getting her back from Portland in June. I'm not sure I would have made it without you."

"No problem, captain."

14

LONDON's Genealogy

It occurs to me one day: *My boat was a boat before she was my boat.*

Suddenly I need to know all about her life before I owned her. Where had she been? What had happened on her deck and in her cabin?

First there is her number. LONDON's hull identification number is CPDJ0035M77F. On the Cape Dory website I learn that *CPD* is the Cape Dory manufacturing code. The next five characters, *J0035*, represent the hull serial number: *J* is a model designation, and *0035* means she was the thirty-fifth 27-foot Cape Dory ever built. The *M* stands for "manufactured," and *77* is the model year. The *F* is the sixth month. The model year starts in August of the previous calendar year, so an *F* means January of 1977.

When I bought LONDON (née LOON) she was owned by two women, Carolyn and Karla. I've met Carolyn, although in a somewhat strained situation since I offered to buy LOON for a lot less than she was asking. Despite our differences over price, I came to respect and like her. During my purchase of the boat we never talked about her experiences on LOON. She did tell me that she once came close to changing the boat's name from LOON to LOON-A-SEA. I am glad she didn't.

I decide to get in touch with Carolyn again. I want to ask her more about my boat's history. I begin by mailing her a letter explaining I have been writing about my experiences with LONDON. I ask if she would be willing to meet with me. I call her a week later and she agrees to meet me for lunch.

In the meantime, I begin to examine LONDON's (LOON's) ancestry by looking through the old papers that came with the boat. Someone named Paul sold the boat to Carolyn. Paul was also from the Boston area. Among the papers I find a copy of LOON's "Consolidated Certificate of Enrollment and Yacht License," issued by the Boston office of the U.S. Coast Guard in February 1980. It is the earliest document I have. I believe it marks the season when LONDON actually hit the water for the first time, even though it seems late for a 1977 boat. I believe this certificate is the original basis of her documentation record.

LONDON was documented when I bought her. In the process of the purchase, the documentation was changed to record me as the new legal owner. Boat documentation is a federal registration that provides evidence of a vessel's nationality and ownership.

The act of documenting a boat was established by the First Federal Congress of the United States, which met in the old Federal Hall on the corner of Wall and Nassau Streets in New York City at the beginning of 1789. Because huge debts remained from the Revolutionary War, one of the major issues on the Congress's agenda was revenue. Early revenue came from tariffs on trade, and these tariff rates were determined by a vessel's nationality. Documentation established the nationality of a vessel. The Coasting Act, passed by August 1789, established the procedures and forms for vessel identification[17].

The Coasting Act was one of four bills that established the federal revenue system. The Impost and Tonnage Bills raised revenues; the Collection and Coasting Bills provided for their enforcement. The need for enforcement led to the creation of a federal bureaucracy and in 1790 the establishment of the U.S. Coast Guard and ten revenue cutters. Until very recently the Coast Guard remained a part of the U.S. Department of the Treasury.

Two of the modern requirements for documentation are that a boat be more than 5 Net Tons and that the owner be a citizen of the United States. Net tonnage is a measurement of volume, not weight. LONDON is recorded on her certificate as being 6 Net Tons[18]. Documented vessels must also be marked in a specific fashion. The documentation number must be displayed in 3-inch-high numbers and permanently attached to the hull. For a recreational boat, the name and hailing port must appear on the stern in letters at least 4 inches high.

I also order an "Abstract of Title" for LONDON for $25 from the National Vessel Documentation Center (N.V.D.C.) in Falling Waters, West Virginia. One morning I arrive at work to find the document has arrived by fax from the N.V.D.C.

The report records each time the boat changed hands, was mortgaged, etc. The first owner was Paul, who bought the boat new from a yacht broker in Marblehead for $39,735.95 at the end of May 1980. Carolyn would later tell me that the boat had spent some time in a warehouse in Marblehead before Paul bought her. So it does look like LONDON first went in the water in the spring of 1980. Paul sold the boat to Carolyn during the fall of 1981 for $26,000. I would buy her from Carolyn and Karla in late September 1998 for $10,500.

On a November morning I drive along Quincy Shore Drive and look out over the part of Quincy Bay where LOON was moored when Carolyn owned her. The water is calm, like a big gray sheet. Fog hides the harbor islands. Carolyn's house is just a few doors up from the bay. She tells me that when her father bought the place, there was nothing between them and the water. He was told he didn't have to worry about anyone building around him. It was all marsh. That apparently didn't stop the developers. It is now a densely populated Boston suburb, but with a pleasant sea breeze.

Carolyn is working at her computer when I arrive. She is a strong, lean woman perhaps sixty-eight years old. Before we leave for the restaurant she shows me her oil painting of LOON. Next to LOON is a painting of another sailboat her family had owned, a Thunderbird. My friend Pete, who lives in Quincy, had also been a Thunderbird sailor, and when I tell her about him she remembers his name from her racing days. Hanging beneath the Thunderbird painting, on her nautical wall, is a needlepoint of the Boston Harbor Islands.

"Dad worked for railway express but when he retired, he built and repaired boats. We are from Nova Scotia. I have always sailed and been around boats. LOON, well your LONDON, is the first boat we owned that we had not built."

On the way to the restaurant Carolyn tells me that she spends three months each year doing construction work under the auspices of her church. For the last few years she has been working on camp buildings in Mississippi and Texas. Locally she works for Habitat for Humanity.

I ask her about the day she bought LOON. What happened? What was it like?

"He didn't say much, but I think that man had a tear in his eye. I don't think he wanted to sell her. He had to move to Washington, D.C. I went over there to Winthrop, to that yacht club, and sailed her back with Karla, Jim, and Jean. We came back by going outside Boston Light. There were groundswells out there, we were going up and down. Jean and Karla had the best time riding up in the bow. I belonged to the Squantum Yacht Club on Quincy Bay. We kept LOON on a mooring in a hole we knew about out there. A nice 7-foot spot."

Carolyn looks out the window at the Marina Bay docks and then back at me. She is smiling now.

"Did you know your boat was hit by lightning? Yup. Second or third year we had her. I was told by someone who knows about electricity that the lightning came down the mast looking for the radio, but we always took the radio ashore because we'd been robbed out there before, so when the lightning didn't find the radio it went back along the wires and blew out the electrical panel. Completely exploded it. My mother had knit afghans for Karla and me. The switches blown from the electrical panel were so hot they melted little holes in the afghans where they landed.

"I had to go up the mast and replace all the lights. They were just welded. It left a crack you know—on the deck, where the lightning went through. There was no one on the boat, thank goodness."

I have noticed the cracked deck. My surveyor thought it might have been made by someone dropping something like a hammer while up the mast. I ask Carolyn if they had ever run LOON aground.

"Well, I guess we did once, in Green Harbor. You been in there? No? We had gone in and there was a dredge there. In the morning we were going out with the fishermen passing us by on both sides. It was half tide. We were right in the middle of that channel and we just stopped. Then the tide just swung us across the channel, so nobody was going in or out. The fishermen gave us a nudge off and then we were okay. They told us that was why the dredge was still there. They hadn't done such a good job."

We talk about where she had sailed LOON. LOON had been to some of the same places LONDON has, although she said she never went further north than Marblehead or further south than Newport. When cruising they tended to go south. On one trip, after a beautiful sail through Woods Hole, they decided to go into Eel Pond; on their approach they got the sail down but the engine wouldn't start.

"What do we do?" Karla asked Carolyn.

"We get out of here, that's what we do."

They decided to sail across to Vineyard Haven, where Carolyn thought they might be lucky enough to sail up to a mooring. They did get a mooring right off the boatyard. The problem was the starter. It was put on the ferry for New Bedford and came back rebuilt two days later.

They passed through Buzzards Bay again another year.

"The year we lost the America's Cup, we had decided to go down there and see the race. We sailed down to Narragansett Bay. After the races we went over to Cuttyhunk and a big yacht from Chicago anchors right next to us. This boat was full of those sailors who are all dressed up in their blues. The kind of sailors who have crew. And they are watching us: three women on a boat. In the morning it was really blowing. You know if it's blowing hard in the morning, you are going to have a busy day. And I said to Karla, we have to plan this. We are not going to give these guys their laugh for the day.

"So I sat down and thought. I took the anchor line and pulled it back to the stern, and wrapped it around the winch. I told her, since now we are anchored off the stern, and pointing downwind, that I'm going to crank this in and when I tell you, you let that jib out, because I would feel the anchor come free. Right? Well, when it came free I yelled to her and she let out the jib and we were out of there just as pretty as can be.

"It just blew and blew that day. You know where that chunk is missing from the teak rail in the transom? That was from the dinghy running down a wave and slamming into the stern. After that I had to sail off the wind a bit, so we were on a bit of a reach and I am thinking, Where to go? It was very rough. You could only see the masts of other boats when they were in the troughs. I settled on Cataumet. We called ahead on the radio and asked if they had a mooring or a slip. They said both. I asked the other two which they wanted. Pat said she wanted to be as close to land as possible, so we took the slip.

"In the morning they wouldn't let any boats go out. It was that bad. It was another day before we headed home. It was still so bad at each end of the canal you could barely steer. I remember calling home—it took forever to get a line, the radio was so busy—and before I got to say anything I heard my mother call out to the house, 'They're okay!' They must have been worried."

Carolyn's hobby is genealogy. She has a website and her latest project is a family genealogy she has produced and published. This may be why she was willing to talk about LONDON's history.

The Cape Dorys are production boats, made for the mass market. In total there were 277 Cape Dory 27s built between the years 1977 and 1985. The CD27 is just one of a series of boats designed by Carl Alberg for Cape Dory Yachts. All told, Cape Dory built nearly 1,000 Alberg-designed sailboats of nearly the same size between 1974 and 1988: In addition to the 27s, there are 189 CD25Ds, 78 CD26s, and 388 CD28s. And then there are CD30s, CD31s, CD33s, etc[19].

When you are sailing a Cape Dory you are sailing in company, especially in the Buzzards Bay area. We are near where the headquarters of Cape Dory Yachts was located in East Taunton. There are two other CD27s in my home anchorage and at least one other Alberg-designed boat, a beautifully restored Alberg 30.

The CD27 is a relatively heavy boat with moderate sail area. It is known for its comfort and stability at sea, and for the strength of its construction. In one place where I drilled through the hull I measured a solid ½-inch of fiberglass material. The CD27 is a simple boat. My engine is a single-cylinder diesel that has proven to be reliable. I have no shower, hot water heater, pressurized water system, or refrigerator to worry about. The boat is a sloop with roller furling on the genoa and two reef points on the mainsail.

The beam of 8.5 feet is relatively narrow for her length, and this is reflected in her initial tenderness, but she firms up quickly. LONDON's hull speed is 6 knots. On a breezy day, with the big genoa out and one reef in the main, she will reach 6.5 knots for short spurts as measured by the GPS. Her capsize ratio is 1.74, which is considered safe. The sail area–displacement ratio is 15.24, which is considered good for a cruising boat, but her displacement–waterline length ratio is 419, quite heavy.

The only criticism I have read of her design is that because her rudder is raked forward, it pulls the stern down when off center and acts as a brake. I have certainly learned that to get the best speed out of LONDON I need to avoid weather helm. Reefing early will actually cause the boat to accelerate. I start to think about reefing when the wind is about 17 knots.

LONDON's designer Carl Alberg designed more than fifty boats. His pioneering 1959 design for the 28-foot Triton produced the first affordable fiberglass cruising sailboat, and in the process launched Pearson Yachts. He would design boats for Cape Dory, Pearson, Bristol, Whitby, and others during his lifetime. About his design philosophy Alberg said, "In all my designs I go for comfortable accommodations and a boat you can sail upright without scaring the life out of your family or friends. I gave them a good long keel, plenty of displacement and beam, and a fair amount of sail area so they can move[20]."

Born in Sweden in 1900, Alberg studied boat design in Sweden before coming to the United States in 1925. He worked with John Alden for a time, and was also a marine engineer and designer for the U.S. Coast Guard. He retired from the Coast Guard in 1963 and began to work with Andrew Vavolotis at Cape Dory Yachts, first designing the CD28. He would design ten boats for Cape Dory. Alberg died in Marblehead, Massachusetts on August 31, 1986.

Cape Dory Yachts ceased operations in the early 1990s, when the entire industry was struggling. The name and many of the molds were sold. Vavolotis moved to Maine and established Robinhood Marine, which continues to build a few selected models based on Cape Dory designs. Robinhood was kind enough to send me a copy of the Builders Certificate for LONDON, which they still had on file. It is dated July 11, 1978 and states that she was built in 1977 for the yacht dealer in Marblehead.

15

In the Cabin

A home that is stable without being stationary, shaped less like
a box than like a fish or a bird or a girl
  —E.B. White, *The Sea and the Wind That Blows*

LONDON's main cabin measures 8 feet, 2 inches across at its widest point. From the aft bulkhead, where the companionway opens into the cockpit, to the forward bulkhead of the main cabin is 6 feet, 6 inches. Headroom is 5 feet, 11 inches at the highest point, but closer to 5 feet, 8 inches near the doorway forward.

Upon boarding the boat I sit on the bridge deck at the forward edge of the cockpit to undo the combination lock, slide the companionway cover forward under its sea hood, slip the three heavy teak washboards up and out of their grooves, and lay them on the deck. This opens the vertical part of the companionway. I can then hop down the companionway steps into the cabin. A center aisle runs down the cabin from the bottom of these steps. The bunks, which also serve as seats, line the sides. At the far end is a small table, offset to the port side. Also at the forward end of the center aisle is a door leading to the head compartment and then forward to the V-berth sleeping area in the bow. Over the V-berth is a large deck hatch, which fills the whole area with fresh sea air. After I stow the companionway boards, I typically open the hatch to air out the interior. The door forward is always left open unless someone is seeking the little privacy to be found down here by closing it. There is plenty of privacy for one person, but not really enough to share.

Nancy and I sometimes refer to the forward V-berth as the "other stateroom," but this is a joke. The spaces below are comfortable and cozy but lack the qualities of both "state" and "room." It is more of a happy, seagoing nest, well stocked for almost any situation.

This main cabin serves as galley, navigation station, sleeping cabin, dining room, pantry, engine room, library, shop, and storeroom. When I am seated on the starboard bunk, the outside water level is about even with my midriff. When prone on the bunk, one of my favorite sailing positions, I am actually below the level of the water outside the boat. Being beneath the surface contributes to the calming and cooling effects of the ocean water on the resting brain. It shields the person reclining from disturbing vibrations and emanations found above the water's surface.

From this position I have been able to hear some of the mysterious noises of the sea echoing through the wet skin of LONDON's fiberglass hull. There is one sound in particular I listen for. Anchored in certain warm water harbors in midsummer I hear a staccato tapping I attribute to "underwater woodpeckers." *Rat-a-tat-tat. Rat-a-tat-tat.* These stereo echoes give LONDON's cabin the feeling of an aquarium—it is like being in the tank with the fish. I sometimes wish that, in addition to the four bronze-rimmed oval portholes that look out at the sky above, the main cabin had a submarine porthole through which I could watch what was going on below the waves while eating my dinner.

A countertop runs across the entire aft area of the cabin. The center of the counter, immediately below the companionway, is a ribbed piece of heavy teak that serves both as a countertop for food preparation (it is located between the sink and stove) and as the top step of the stairs into the cabin. This is a combination usage I encourage the more hygienic of my guests to ignore. Underneath this top step and behind the removable stairs is the engine access—carefully designed for a midget with freakishly long and flexible arms.

Cut into the left side of this countertop, as you face aft, is the freshwater sink, and off to the left rear is a large top-opening cooler. A shelf stretches back along the far left wall of the counter surface. This is where I keep my paper towels, plastic containers filled with cutlery, a rich assortment of kitchen utensils, my store of garbage bags, and the Pyrex measuring cup. I now only rarely use the cup since I have established that one full depression of the freshwater foot pump mounted below the sink will always yield exactly ½ cup of water. Mounted on the left bulkhead above the countertop is a teak dish rack. Also here I have two hooks. One, in the corner, is where I hang the garbage bag; the second, high up and just inside the companionway opening, is where I keep a Hoffritz rigging knife (a present from my father-in-law when I first got the boat), my Greek worry beads, a whistle, and a St. Christopher's medal. I keep them all here so that I can reach them from the cockpit. I found the St. Christopher's medal when I first began cleaning the cabin and have religiously kept it in the boat. St. Christopher is the patron saint of travelers and mariners. By coincidence, it is also the name of the Church of England school I attended as an American boy living in England. I recited "Sea Fever" in St. Christopher's gym.

The right side of the aft cabin wall is crowded with stuff. Here the bulkhead is thicker and protrudes a bit into the cabin. The handheld VHF radio is mounted along the inside edge, adjacent to the companionway, so that it too is accessible from the cockpit. Next to it is the main battery switch. The bulkhead itself contains the full set of switches and fuses for the boat's electrical circuits, the fuel and electric meters, the switch and fuse for the automatic bilge pump, and a 12-volt "cigarette lighter" receptacle, which I use to charge the cell phone and my laptop computer. Beneath all of this is a Swedish-built Origo two-burner alcohol stove with a removable cutting board top, and behind it the top-loading dry food lockers.

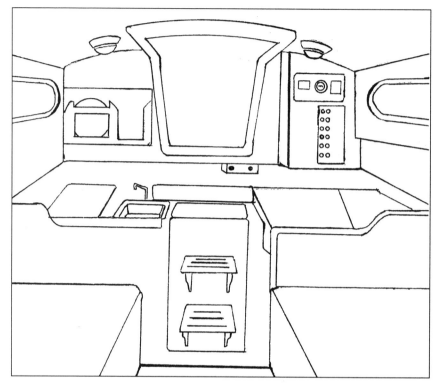

Cabin Interior Looking Aft

The bank of switches is divided into nine circuits. This is the same panel that was blown up when the boat was struck by lightning and later rebuilt. They are:

1. GPS and gauges
2. Anchor light at masthead
3. Running lights
4. Cabin lights
5. Steaming lights
6. Deck light
7. Depth meter
8. VHF radio
9. AM/FM radio and accessory 12-volt plug

The AM/FM radio is mounted under the companionway entrance, and beneath it, tucked against the back of the counter, is a three-pocket shelf. In the first two pockets I keep little bottles of balsamic vinegar and olive oil, salt and pepper shakers, SPF 30 sunblock, a bottle of pure castile soap and— for the less hip—a pump bottle of antibacterial liquid soap, a bottle of Old English lemon oil, which I use in the constant fight against mildew, and a collapsible multi-tool, which I reach for first if I find something loose up above.

The last pocket holds my wind instrument. This neat little handheld gadget measures the wind speed in knots, miles per hour, or kilometers per hour. It is battery-powered, the size of a pack of cigarettes, and has a compact, easy-to-read LCD display showing numbers and a bar graph. It is made of a flexible plastic with a soft, green, fuzzy outer surface that makes it comfortable and perhaps even reassuring to hold. A pop-off top reveals the little flywheel that spins in the wind. It is an economical tool for getting an accurate deck-level wind speed. Also in this pocket is the ship's clock—a drugstore-variety travel clock with an insidious alarm—a corkscrew, bottle openers, a small flashlight with a rubberized outer surface, a Swiss army knife, and finally a single tube of sail track lubricant. This little tube transformed LONDON's sail hoisting and dropping to an easygoing, slippery affair. All of these items, and all of the electrical switches, can be reached by leaning into the cabin from the cockpit.

Above each bunk, vertical wooden paneling creates shallow storage lockers against the curve of the hull and supports a long shelf above. The shelf runs the full length of the bunk, some 6 feet, tapering with the shape of the hull. The average width is perhaps 4 inches, with a 4-inch-deep fiddle edge to keep items from falling out. This long, trough-like shelf is both useful and perplexing. Things collect behind the fiddle edge and can only be found by feel—the shape of the deck and cabintop make it impossible to view the contents of the shelf from above. When I put things here, I try to make a mental note of their location. The alternative is to find them by walking my hand through the contents from one end to the other.

All the way aft on the starboard shelf I keep my clothespins and a supply of light yacht braid. Moving forward, the next item is a clear, compartmentalized box of rigging bits and pieces: bolts, cotter pins, tiny blocks, split rings, and an assortment of clevis pins. Next I find two small spools of electrical wire and then one of my favorite items, a planisphere, about 12 inches in diameter.

I love maps and charts of all kinds, and the planisphere is the sky chart I use the most. It consists of a mask with an oval-shaped opening which rotates above a star chart. I use the time and date scale on the outside of the wheel to dial the mask into position and reveal a custom star map of what is currently overhead. The outer edge of the oval window represents the horizon and is marked with the points of the compass. The center of the oval corresponds to the celestial zenith.

The boat makes a great platform for stargazing by eye and with binoculars; there is too much motion to use a telescope. If you sail at night just a few miles off the coast of Massachusetts, away from land-based sources of light pollution, you can see the Milky Way. On the ocean the sky is bigger, the horizons further away, the celestial sphere immense.

There is some distortion between the printed representation of the sky on the little, flat planisphere and the huge dome of the sky. I find it easiest to face in a certain direction, say east, and then hold the planisphere in front of me with east facing down, similar to how you would use a chart. In my logs are descriptions of star finding that read like navigation of a nautical kind:

August 9, 2002, 1:20 A.M. , Tarpaulin Cove
Again a shooting star. The night is a bit hazier tonight, but the sky is still
fantastic—Milky Way clear. Get out the star map and look for the Great
Square of Pegasus, then I find the star known as Alpha Andromedae, and
move along an arc to Beta Andromedae, turn 90 degrees and run down
her leg and there almost overhead is the Andromeda galaxy, 2.5 million

light years away, a dim blur of gaseous disk in my binoculars. In the east some of the more familiar winter constellations are beginning to rise. More meteors.

August 12, 2002, 2:45 A.M. , Hadley Harbor
Tonight is the night of the shooting stars! Been watching the Perseid meteor shower and again looked at Andromeda. One meteor made a broad golden streak and then blew up in a sudden flash that made me blink.

  Lay on deck and look straight up into Cassiopeia in the Milky Way. Boat slowly drifting back and forth on anchor rope making stars swing by overhead. Water laps against hull. Deck damp with dew. It strikes me that the patterns we have made with the star charts are much like the patterns on the navigational charts. Star charts / sea charts.

  Picking my way through New Bedford outer harbor I was looking for a reference point—something clearly recognizable as I came in from the bay. First the radome and then the big bell at the Sandspit were what I fixed on. From them I found and went past the smaller nun at Great Ledge, which led to the other nuns off North Ledge. I do the same thing looking at the stars between meteors. I pick a reference point, a distant mark I can trust, and work my way across the sky from there, navigating from the Great Square of Pegasus point to point in an arc to find the Andromeda galaxy.

I think of the planisphere as marking the beginning of the "Science Section" of the cabin shelf. Next come books, first the field guides: the *National Audubon Society Field Guide to North American Fishes, Whales, and Dolphins*; the *National Audubon Society Field Guide to the Night Sky*; a Peterson field guide to the Atlantic seashore; *A Field Guide to Sailboats*; and the *National Audubon Society Field Guide to North American Birds*.

Not long ago I made use of the *Atlantic Seashore Guide* on the water. I had taken Bruce and his friend, their two daughters, each named Katherine, and Bruce's son John out for our now-annual summer sail. It was breezy and the cockpit was crowded. I left the main down and just floated the genoa. We took a quick sail and pulled into the lee of West Island in Buzzards Bay to anchor, eat, and jump off the

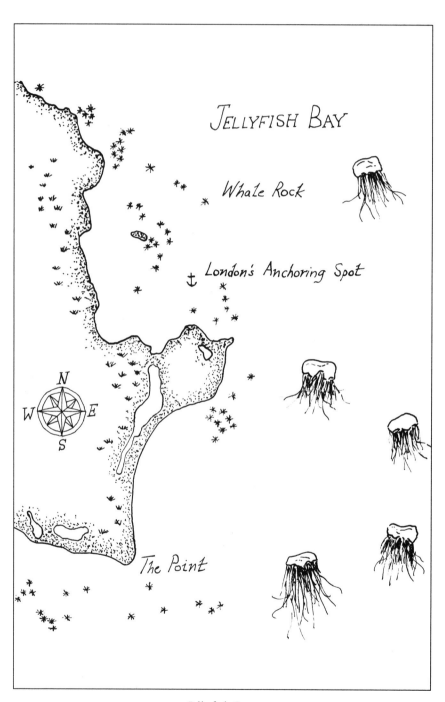

Jellyfish Bay

boat into the water. The kids soon spotted numerous big jellyfish
floating out of the bay, as if in schools. We took the dinghy ashore
and waded into a warm tidal creek, about 3 feet deep, that was roaring out from the inner lagoon. We waded along it, picking at the
golden shells, and then floated on the racing current round the bend
where it cut through the marsh grass and then accelerated across the
beach and into the bay. We all took this ride at least four times. We
soon had a bunch of very happy and excited kids.

"I don't know why I didn't want to come here," says one young
Katherine.

"I think this has been the best day of my whole life!" says the
other.

Later, after they have all left, I look up the jellyfish that had
drifted by LONDON all day in *The Atlantic Seashore*, a field guide by
Kenneth Gosner. They are called Lion's Mane or Red Jelly, *Cyanea
capillata*: "A large jellyfish with broad, flattish bell, and numerous
mouth-arms and tentacles below." The Lion's Mane is the largest
jellyfish in the world; they are common and appear all along this
coast. We often had several in view from the deck at once. Their
caps undulated in the water as they passed by the anchored boat just
below the surface[21].

These jellyfish are annuals. They reach their full size in a single
summer season and then die. In its youth (called the *ephyra* stage) the
jellyfish is said to be secretive. The floating *ephyra* have broken off
from a polyp, which was in turn attached to eel grass or another
shallow water structure. The adult jellyfish are invertebrate animals
and carnivorous, stinging their prey with their long tentacles. In
both stages the jellyfish has an eight-part structured underbody.
This jellyfish makes an appearance in the Sherlock Holmes mystery
"The Lion's Mane":

"Cyanea!" I cried. "Cyanea! Behold the Lion's Mane!"

In true nineteenth-century fashion, Sherlock and his companions
crushed the specimen they had found in a tide pool by rolling a large
rock onto it after deducing it has stung a man to death. There was

a lot of talk on my boat that afternoon about whether or not we would be stung by swimming into the jelly. There were no volunteers to make a conclusive experiment. According to the *National Audubon Society Field Guide to New England*, this was fortunate. In its discussion of the jellyfish that book includes the warning, "Caution: Highly toxic; causes severe burns, blisters; can be fatal[22]." Other sources I found later described the jellyfish as merely irritating. I remain unsure as to the potency of their sting.

A bright yellow paperback, the *Eldridge Tide and Pilot Book—2002*, is next on the shelf. I keep it here where I can reach it from my bunk while sailing, but it also goes in my boat bag to go home with me when I go ashore. This book contains all the tide and current information for the area for the upcoming year. I use it regularly for trip planning. Again from the log:

> *September 7, 2002, 8:00 A.M. , Katama Bay*
> *I read the Eldridge Tide and Pilot Book the way my nephew Jon reads baseball statistics. It is a kind of relaxation to pore through the stats and build up a picture of the next day—what's happening with the tide and currents at Pollock Rip, Woods Hole, and the canal. This along with the marine weather forecast may help to determine what I will attempt, where I will go. It is only now with my fourth copy of Eldridge down here that the Vineyard currents are beginning to make sense.*

After the books is a blue plastic box. It sits at an angle in the shelf, not quite fitting. It contains the engine ignition key, the deck keys for the water and waste access, dowels, padlock keys, nails, and a button. Finally, there is a small stash of matches sealed against moisture, a fishing rod and reel, and the mainsail's batten-loosening tool.

On the corresponding shelf above the opposite bunk, at the aft end, is a red plastic box that contains my fire sources—boxes of matches and all the cigarette lighters I have confiscated from my daughters and their friends. Next is a pair of very loud handheld air horns, a collapsible hanging candle holder with candle, a pencil sharpener, pencils and pens, and two pairs of parallel rules.

Moving forward along the port shelf we encounter the flag staff and rolled-up flag, hats, and a turkey baster. The hats are of two types: the large, floppy cotton canvas sunscreening type, and the knit caps that keep your head warm. I am bald. Protecting my head from the sun and the cold are essential, so hat selection is a big deal. The boat usually has four or five hats aboard. I lose at least one hat a year to a wind gust. The hats that do fly off my head always seem to have slipped below the surface of the waves and out of the reach of my boathook by the time I have executed a quick stop and returned. I hope anyone who falls off my boat will manage to stay afloat for a bit longer. Since we are usually towing an inflatable, LONDON's crew know that the first thing to do if someone goes overboard is to let loose the inflatable. It can serve both as a marker and as a float for a person in the water.

Other than giving me a chance to practice the quick stop, my hats serve a second purpose: scalp protection. Hair on the top of the head acts as a contact early-warning system, much as a cat's whiskers do. Most full-haired people do not appreciate this. Once the hair is gone there is no warning and the most awful collisions can occur between the scalp and any solid object. People with hair have just enough time after feeling a sensation through the strands of their hair to stop or at least slow their head motion, while baldies blindly slam into the object and cut their scalps open. This was a big problem for me when I first got LONDON. I always seemed to have a scab running across my scalp. I eventually learned that wearing a hat when I had my head stuck in the cockpit lockers or the engine compartment would give me the same warning and protection as a head of hair. My scalp was able to heal.

Before I acquired the turkey baster I used to spill stove fuel. The alcohol stove on LONDON has cylindrical canisters packed with a cotton-like batten. These are soaked with alcohol to fuel the stove. Pouring the alcohol through a funnel into the canister is a tricky business. Inevitably the alcohol pours out of the container too quickly, overflows, and spills before it can be absorbed by the cotton.

The turkey baster is the 98-cent solution. I now baste the alcohol slowly into the stove.

At the end of the port shelf lie a spare winch handle, extra sail ties, my water sandals, and a roll of masking tape. Above this end of the shelf is where the VHF radio now hangs. I have bought a replacement for this old unit and plan to install it near the companionway so that I can reach it from the cockpit.

Beneath these long shelves are the storage lockers between the hull wall and the bunk backs. On the starboard side, this compartment has two hatches. Behind the aft hatch I keep all my pots and pans; behind the forward one are cruising guides and books on boat maintenance and seamanship.

On the port side there is only a single hatch in the vertical bunk back. In this compartment I keep my two inflatable life jackets, one with a harness tether, two strap harnesses and tethers, the auto-tiller, and LONDON's plug-in spotlight.

I have modified access to the lockers under the bunks by adding top-opening hatches. After pulling the bunk cushion up and out of the way, one can now easily reach down into that space. Previously they were only accessible through an inconvenient door in the lower aisle wall. I have divided the starboard under-bunk locker into fore and aft sections with a plywood and epoxy wall. The forward section makes up a small, clean locker I use for all my papers, manuals and small electronics—handheld GPS, current inverter, spare anchor light.

The aft portion is filled with tools and toolboxes. There is a set of open stainless steel wrenches, a cheap socket wrench kit in a plastic case, a yellow toolbox in which I keep all my electric bits (fuses, bits of wire, connectors, a digital multi-tester, a crimping tool, bulbs, etc.), and an old blue tackle box in which I keep many of my favorite items: stubby regular and Phillips head screwdrivers, pliers, bits of wire, cotter pins, machine screws and washers, and many other fasteners. Also under here is the diesel fill funnel in an oily rag, the metric wrench set, and the spares for the Yanmar diesel: the impeller, fuel filters, and belts.

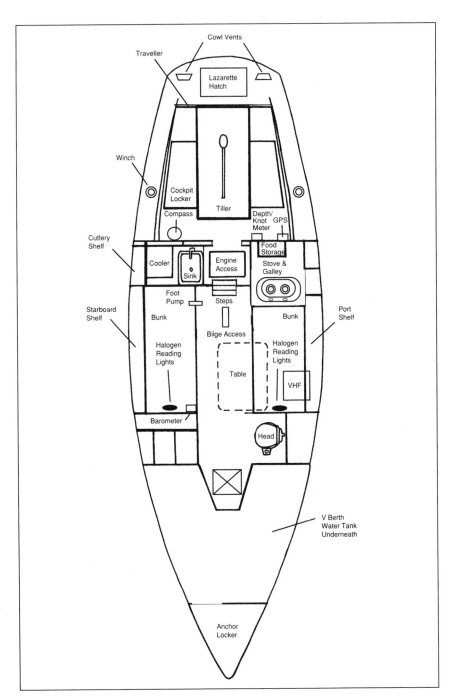

LONDON Layout

In the opposite under-bunk compartment are tools less often used and emergency equipment. A hammer and the soft wood plugs for all the through-hulls are here, as is a hack saw in a sealed plastic bag. The sail repair items are in another plastic bag: wax, needles, thread, sailcloth, corks, awl, and sail tape. A solid plastic cylinder is used to store a backup supply of slightly out-of-date flares (nine red, one orange smoke). A flat solid case contains the up-to-date flare pistol and seven charges, as well as a whistle, a mirror reflector, and a glow stick. A second round tube puzzled me when I pulled it out of this locker recently. It was taped around the middle and clearly labeled "Clamps & Tubes." I knew what I had meant by clamps, but tubes? Was this extra hose? No, that couldn't be: The extra lengths of hose are forward under the peak of the V-berth. I opened it to find tubes of winch grease, marine silicone caulk, 3M 4200 polyurethane sealant, 3M 5200 polyurethane adhesive sealant, and the traditional 101 polysulfide bedding compound. The last few items in this locker are my mosquito head net, a box of fishing tackle, flippers, swim mask, and snorkel.

I keep the charts I am not using under the cushions of both bunks in large plastic bags. This keeps them flat and easily accessible.

On the starboard side of the forward bulkhead of the main cabin is my barometer; on the port side is a hook on which I hang my light foul-weather jacket. Also on this side of the cabin I have a string of Tibetan prayer flags my sister and Bill gave me. I string them the length of the cabin for good luck and color.

A black-framed picture of the city of London on the King's Birthday in 1775 decorates the space between the two bronze oval portholes on the port side. A river scene showing a frigate decorated with flags at anchor in front of the Tower of London. It seemed just right.

16

Sounding Katama Bay

The weather forecast is perfect. Cool, sunny, and dry. Clear nights. New moon. Big tides.

Sailing off Martha's Vineyard I switch over to the auto-tiller, head LONDON into the wind, and walk up to the mast to drop the mainsail. As I am folding the sail I watch the boats behind me in the channel begin to catch up and then pass by. The sun is warm but it won't be for much longer. I can make out the Edgartown Harbor jetty ahead. For the last hour or so, the thermal breezes off the shore were finally enough to move the boat, but otherwise the wind has been fitful and weak all day, less than forecast. To get here before dark I used the engine to push through an ebb tide for much of the afternoon.

The narrow passage through the town of Edgartown is the prettiest such channel in New England. The spire of the Old Whaling Church dominates the tumble of village structures along the west shore. I see a schooner tied up at the town dock taking on passengers, while a fleet of small boats bustles around the waterfront. Just ahead of me the Chappy ferries pass one another in mid-channel, like two chickens endlessly crossing and recrossing the road.

After the ferries and the sharp turn in the channel, the town moorings come up quickly on the port side. The blue-topped ones are first-come, first-served; the yellow ones further along the channel can be reserved through the harbormaster. The prices are reasonable, especially considering what they get now over in Nantucket.

LONDON glides through the water, leaving Edgartown astern and continuing down the channel into Katama Bay. I make a slow circle well past the cluster of larger anchored boats. I keep one eye on the depth meter. It registers a steady 8 feet. The tide is near low. *Auto* holds the tiller amidships. I take LONDON out of gear aimed into the wind. As she slows, I walk to the bow, drop the 25-pound CQR over the side, and tie it off with 70 feet of line. It is a big anchor for the boat.

"It's like throwing a Volkswagen over the side."

I look around. No one is close enough to hear. I am talking to myself again.

Out of habit I look to both sides to memorize my anchor spot according to landmarks on shore, but mostly I take in the scene. The near shore is dominated by large homes but to the south, across an open expanse of calm shoal water, I clearly see the barrier beach, all that separates the bay from the open force of the Atlantic Ocean. I will dinghy over there in the morning. An osprey passes overhead. A light breeze ruffles the water surface and carries the warm scent of pitch pine out to me.

I congratulate myself on such a quiet, easy anchorage (always a bad sign) and go below to open a bottle of red wine chilled in the cooler and begin to cook dinner. Dinner is "Annie's Shells & White Cheddar." I mix in chunks of juicy tomatoes from my garden and coarse black pepper. This is a regular item on the evening boat menu. Sleep comes early.

I awake suddenly. It is totally dark and surprisingly cold. I pull my sleeping bag up around me. I don't want to get up. By the glowing dial of the ship's clock I can see it is a little after 2:00 in the morning. There is no moon. Then I feel it again. As if something was brushing against the bottom of the boat. Through the open companionway I watch the stars sweep across the night sky as the boat swings on her anchor.

We are moving, so we are still afloat. What did I feel?

Even dimwitted with sleep, or just plain dimwitted, I know I need to investigate or I will lie here all night waiting for the next bump. I pull on my clothes. I see my hands are shivering as I reach across the cabin to flick on the instruments. It is only the three steps from the cabin up to the cockpit, but my legs are heavy.

"Hah! Ten feet. Just as I would have expected."

I look up from the depth meter and watch the stars, until out of the corner of my eye I see the numbers on the display begin a descent. My heart races as the numbers drop—8 feet, 6 feet, 4 feet, down to an incredible 2.6 feet, 2.5 feet, 2.4 feet, and then "- -." I brace myself for the bump of the boat against the bottom. Nothing happens. The meter jumps back to 10 feet.

"What the heck?"

The croak of a heron disturbs the stillness, then the beating of wet wings. The depth meter continues to read 10 feet. I want to get back in the sleeping bag. I try to dismiss what I have just seen as a flight of imagination, or an instrument aberration. It doesn't work. The engineer in me has taken over. The calculations and observations begin.

The boat draws 4 feet. The depth meter displays the actual depth from the surface of the water. So we should float in anything over a 4-foot reading. In addition, I have added a fudge factor of 2 feet: Even if the depth meter reads 4 feet, I still have an extra 2 feet under the keel, the real depth being 6 feet.

We would not actually touch bottom until the meter read 2 feet. Theoretically. But to see the reading go from 2 feet to nothing at all, yet still be afloat—it is too much for my sleepy brain. I go get a blanket. This is going to take a while.

I arrange the cushions in the cockpit so I can lie down on the narrow fiberglass seat. I line up the boat with the lights on shore and watch to see if the low readings occur at the same spot as the boat swings back and forth on the arc of her anchor line. If there is a regular pattern, it may indicate a shallow spot or a rock or some other obstruction under the boat. I pull the blanket over my legs.

As usual, the wind has shifted direction since sunset, so I am hanging over a different part of the bottom than when I dropped the anchor. If I knew where this shallow spot was, I could move the boat a bit. I am loath to move the boat in the dark without knowing where I am going. I have done that before, in Maine. It only led to more trouble. If I had a fish-finder, I could "see" the bottom. That would be cool.

I lie there for an hour, lining up lights left on ashore, waiting for the boat to swing, and watching the meter. I see the readings descend in the same way as before and then jump back to 10, but there is no pattern as to when this occurs. No particular spot consistently reads shallow. I am beginning to wonder about fish or underwater floating debris interfering with the readings when the meter settles down for an extended stay in the low 2s. I reach for the 8-foot telescoping boathook, extend it all the way, and plunge it into the water around the boat, reaching as deep as I can. There is nothing there. I cannot touch bottom. I stow the boathook, turn off the instruments, and go back to bed, thinking of the greenish phosphorescent glow the boathook excited in the warm, black water. I am asleep again in minutes.

In the morning I can feel from the boat's motion that we are still afloat. I slip on some pants, flip on the instruments, and go on deck to look at the depth meter. It reads "- -." I realize I must have spent an hour or more last night watching the freakish death of the depth meter. I am not pleased, for several reasons.

One, without a depth meter I can't do the gunkholing around Nantucket Sound I had planned. I will need to stay in deep water.

Two, I had installed the instrument myself only two years ago, to much personal congratulation. The depth meter the boat had come with, which was some twenty years old, had one of those extruding transducers mounted in a tapered block of teak. I suspected this projection from the hull might have snagged the lobster pot warp off Portsmouth, New Hampshire a few years back, leading me to call the Coast Guard for the one and only time in my sailing life. When the old depth finder became erratic, I was eager to replace it with a new instrument, and I chose a transducer that could be mounted inside the hull. In the winter, while the boat was ashore, I unfastened the old transducer and knocked it out of the boat with one satisfying pop of a big sledge hammer. I ground the fiberglass hull around the hole to taper it into a surface the epoxy could grip. Once the hole was fiberglassed over, I sanded the new surface smooth and installed the new transducer on the inside of the hull where the hole had been.

It was a good transducer, well designed to deal with the critical problem of getting the transducer base aligned with the sea bottom, not the slope of the hull. Once the boat was back in the water, I tested the readings from the depth finder against sounding-line measurements in shallow water and then against the chart in deeper water. Rich and I had seen it register 399 feet in the Gulf of Maine, before it maxed out. It had given me two seasons of perfect service, and now this.

Three, it occurs to me that I should have thought to reach and poke around under the boat with the boathook a lot sooner instead of blindly trusting the instrument. I had installed the instrument. I had tested it. I trusted it. There's a mistake.

While waiting for the morning to warm up for my excursion to the beach, I open up the back of the instrument panel to check the one connection in the transducer circuit. It is dry, clean, and shining. No problem there. I turn the instrument on and off several times. Nothing. Time to go to the beach. I will think of something later. Perhaps.

In the inflatable I motor along the west shore of the Katama Bay through the moored boats, and once past them I find the private channel markers that lead to the public ramp. I stop the outboard, tilt it up out of the water, and drop my little dinghy anchor to leave my boat with the others anchored off the launch ramp. I wade ashore with the intention of following the road around to the beach, but once out on the road I am suddenly in suburbia. New, gray-shingled houses sit on regular brown grass lots. I walk past two houses and decide this is not what I want to do. It is hot and somehow boring. I hurry back to the dinghy.

As I pass back through the boat ramp parking lot, I take in the scene. Eight large steel shipping containers have been dropped here.

Their doors are open and plastered with sporty sailing logos. The inside of the containers have been customized to hold disassembled high-performance racing catamarans, which are just now being dragged out and assembled on the grass. Foil sails lie unfurled near the flagpole. A guy with a ponytail and beard is fastening shrouds to an incredibly thin, light hull. It gleams in the sun, a perfect unblemished white. Among the huge shipping containers, there are deck chairs and umbrellas. A young woman in a bathing suit lazes in one chair absorbed in a paperback. Everyone is young, good-looking, and athletic. The whole place has the air of a movie set. I have stumbled into the staging area for the upcoming 2002 A-Class Catamaran World Championships. There are teams here from Austria, Germany, Switzerland, the United States, and other countries. I have seen catamarans racing by on the bay and outside in Vineyard Sound. One blew by when I arrived at Edgartown yesterday at what seemed like thirty knots, feverishly chased by a high-performance red inflatable.

I wade back to my inflatable, neither high-performance nor red, and heave myself up over its gray tube. I leave the motor out of the water and row across the shallows toward the back of South Beach with the little plastic paddles that pass as oars. My feet dry in the sunshine. Near the beach I spot a family. The kids are picking at something in the warm, wet sand. I keep paddling along the shore and land near a tall post. A path leads through the dunes. I emerge on an open ocean beach. There is a seal watching me from the surf. It is just him and me. We are happy. Well, at least I am. He just looks happy. Seals have only one expression.

I am reminded of another line from a Masefield poem, this one from "Harbour Bar": "The white line of the running surf goes booming down the beach."

Sandpipers run in frantic groups along the shore while schools of bluefish feed just outside the breaking waves. Birds swirl and dive from overhead to steal little fish from the surface of the sea. I use my binoculars to watch the boats trolling around Muskeget Channel and out across the adjacent shoals. When the seal is gone, I go for a swim.

After a couple of hours I go back to my anchored sailboat and get into the water to scrub algae off the boat's boot stripe. I then go back to what I have been thinking about, the depth finder. I dive under the boat to see if anything has plastered itself to the hull where the transducer is located. I don't know exactly what I expect to see—some sudden marine growth or perhaps an adhesive jelly creature, one that is excited and attracted by the short high-frequency pulses of sound emanating from just this section of my hull. I find nothing, dry off, and take a nap.

In the evening, while cooking, I watch two racing catamarans maneuvering around my boat to tack upwind. Others coming in from Vineyard Sound just fly across the bay tilted up on one hull. Dinner is wheat pilaf with a can of green beans, another boat staple. Dessert is a few sections of bittersweet chocolate. After dessert I make a crude lead-line with a fishing weight and some light yacht braid. I tie knots every five feet. This will be my backup. I take a reading with my line: 11 feet of water.

I am talking to my wife on the cell phone when a great blue heron slides across the bay about 6 inches above the surface. Later, after dark, I am brought on deck again by the sound of splashing. I shine the beam of my flashlight into the water around the boat. We are surrounded by an enormous school of 2-inch-long minnows. My flashlight seems to attract them until a dull white shape, almost like an underwater cloud, emerges from below and they scatter across the surface. I look up. Scorpius is setting in the west—like the summer. I will head home tomorrow.

The next evening back on my home mooring, I begin to miss the boat even before I step into the inflatable for the quick ride to the dock. I see other sailors are hurrying to get off their boats and back to their cars, their homes, their jobs, their lives. A plastic cooler is passed over a transom to a husband standing in a dinghy. Another sailor straightens a sail cover and then starts the outboard; his wife puts the boards in the companionway and they start for the dock. The breeze is beginning to feel cooler. I reach for a fleece jacket. The sputter of outboards drones over the water in the growing dark.

On the dock conversations are quick. We all want to talk, but everyone is in a hurry, captured again by the impatient land. I am no different. A quick wave, a few short hurried sentences, and I am in my car headed north, thinking of my family, whom I have not seen in three days.

The next morning I awake to sunlight pouring in between the tall green pines behind my house and through the large window into our room, the air fresh with the smell of the woods. I get up early with my wife and daughter, see them off to work and school, and over breakfast begin to think it would be a good day to drive back down to the boat and take another look at that depth finder. It is only 86 miles from door to dock. Maybe there will be time for a sea trial if I get it working again. I take a container of mineral oil out of the kitchen cabinet and go.

I am back at the boat by 10:30 A.M. and begin to take apart the bunk above the transducer. Once I have clear access to the transducer, I unscrew its outer cover and stare in at the mechanism. I find the installation manual under the other bunk and after looking at the diagrams remember that this transducer has a bayonet mount—it just twists off. I remove it and peer into the well that should be full of mineral oil. It is nearly dry. The mineral oil acts as an acoustic conductor between the surface of the transducer and the fiberglass hull below. I fill it again, reassemble it, and turn the depth finder on. On deck I take one look and exclaim, "Yes!" I make a mental note to top this off every spring, start the engine, and toss off the mooring line. I am sailing again. I will reassemble the bunk at anchor.

17

LONDON Food

London has long been known as a city of terrible food. How many times have I heard "English food is awful!" delivered with a smirk and a grimace by a friend who visited London in the 1960s or 70s and who, knowing that I once lived there, needs to describe his culinary disappointment. There has been a flavorful renaissance in London restaurants, not that I ever thought the food was as bad as people said. I like those eggs and sausages, fish and chips, those shepherd's pies. I have eaten Spam, spread Bovril on a small slice of wheat bread, washed it all down with orange squash, and wanted more. In any case, the galley of London's floating namesake has never, in my unbiased opinion, suffered from poor food.

The improvement in London's cuisine is often attributed to the number of restaurants now run by people from the continent. On the boat too, it is a foreign taste, slightly spiced, that keeps things interesting. There are some meals I consume so often on LONDON during the summer months that I avoid them for the remainder of the year, just as I used to save Spam as a summer youth-hosteling meal.

LONDON's galley is simple: a two-burner alcohol stove, a large built-in cooler, two dry food lockers, a portable cooler under the table, some counter space, and a cutting board.

In the food lockers, located behind the stove, there are today three bags of cereal: a bag of the Stark Sisters Maple Almond Not-So-Sweet Granola, a box of Kasha, and another cereal mixture in a plastic freezer bag—raisin bran and Cheerios from home. It is my habit to mix my cereals in the morning by picking and choosing from the different packages. If the raspberries in my garden are ripe, I will bring some of these for a cereal garnish. Breakfast is simple. Strong tea with milk. Cereal and fruit. Pita bread with jam. Wash the dishes, get up on deck, and pull up the anchor. I am the slave of an early start.

Also in the lockers are two bags of pita bread, a single bag of chicken-flavored ramen noodles, and two bags of various loose tea bags.

Among the cans are the ubiquitous tuna, diced tomatoes, chili with beans, mushrooms, French-style green beans, baked beans, and one half-used jar of natural creamy peanut butter.

A paper cup-like container with a peel-off top contains a red beans and rice mix, a soupy dish made in its own packaging by adding boiling water and letting it stand ten or fifteen minutes. From New Zealand there are four loose apples, each bearing a sticker declaring its heritage and breeding: one Braeburn and three Royal Galas.

One bag (half-used) of roasted jumbo peanuts, unshelled. I love eating these in the cockpit. The fragile, brown paper-thin flakes of peanut shell collect around the cockpit scuppers and fly through the air and overboard with the broken bits of outer shell to leave a trail we might use to find our way home on a foggy day. Sailing is one of the few sports that allow time for the shelling of nuts (cricket is another).

One organic sesame bar with date syrup and black cumin. This, like most of the organic items listed here, has come from the organic food store where my youngest daughter works. These snack bars are a great nutritional snack without a lot of refined sugars, and I get a discount.

In this same locker we also have boxes: British digestive biscuits, Canadian stoned wheat crackers, shells and cheese mix, quick brown rice mix, falafel mix, hummus mix, two lentil pilaf mixes, hot milk chocolate drink mix, rice pilaf, and one bag of powdered milk.

I keep two cool areas in the boat. There is the original, large, built-in cooler aft starboard, which I no longer fill with ice but use as a cool place to keep drinks, produce, and jam. In here is a bottle of a local Boston-brewed beer (it has been here all summer), twenty-four cans of lemon and lime seltzer, two bottles of an inexpensive but delicious French Rhône wine, and a jar of Swiss mixed berry jam. This cooler also has a top-level ventilated shelf where I keep fruits and vegetables. At the time of this inventory, three juicy red Big Girl tomatoes from my own garden lie here. It could just as easily have been lettuce or cucumbers from the store, oranges, or the always popular banana.

Instead of trying to chill the big cooler with huge chunks of diminishing ice, I now carry on and off the boat a small top-loading plastic cooler that fits between the legs of the cabin table. A sail tie strap strung between the table legs keeps this cooler pressed against the face of the port bunk even when LONDON is heeled over. The small cooler is far better insulated and vastly more efficient. A block of ice will live for days in here during even the hottest weather. The items I try to keep cool are limited. During this food census, the ice-cold cooler contained a quart of skim milk, a bar of cheddar cheese, fragrant dark Provençal olives, a container of plain yogurt, a plastic container of hummus, a container of pad thai, and another of tofu potato curry.

By restricting the amount of food I need to keep cool, I have freed LONDON from regular trips back to some exhaust-ridden strip mall of a port for a reload of ice, or from the heavy electrical power demands of an onboard refrigeration system. Even in midsummer, with this simple system I can go three days and still keep my milk as fresh as that found on a damp Yorkshire dale. After that, there is always the powder. Simple foods for a simple boat—even if they are all imported.

The most common summer lunch on LONDON is a pita bread wrap, and the most common wrap is hummus on pita with good rich olives and slices of fresh tomato. There are variations: Bits of cooked chicken or fish from the previous night, lettuce, or even a curried rice and yogurt mix can also be spread.

There are two choices for dinner. Number one, if in port, go out to eat. Number two, prepare an almost satisfying mixture of pilaf rice and canned green beans, or a whole pot of lentil pilaf, or if conditions are calm enough to allow deep frying, the delicious falafel balls on a pile of cool plain yogurt with bits of fresh tomato and cold peppered noodles on the side. Failing that, there is always shells and cheese.

Then there is foraging. I never forget the bounty of the sea. If you are at Block Island or Cuttyhunk, men in boats will come and press chowder, steamers, and bits of fried fish over the side—for a price. In Rockport, Massachusetts the harbormasters will toss you fresh lobsters, while way down east in Maine I have had fellow sailors heave 4-pound clusters of salty fresh mussels into my cockpit as they sped by on their way to their own steaming pots. Enjoy. Some of it is free.

On this plain boat diet I soon crave sweet things. I keep a chocolate fruit and nut bar hidden somewhere on my boat at all times. Well hidden from my voracious sister, Karen. That way I know that when the sweet craving comes it can be satisfied.

The prepackaged rice and noodle salads, like couscous and pad thai, have saved many a voyage on LONDON. Rich in complex carbohydrates, these dishes can keep you going when it is too rough to cook and no one wants any more pita anything. After these are gone offer digestive biscuits with cheddar cheese, fruit, nuts, and diet Pepsi if you have it—it is an amazing remedy for *mal de mer*. Encourage the patient to burp.

Below are a few of our favorite recipes:

LONDON **Veggie Surprise**

1 package lentil pilaf mix
1 teaspoon curry powder
½ cup chopped onion
2 cups cut green beans
1 cup chopped tomato
½ cup chopped spinach
¾ cup shredded cheese

A typical one-pot meal. Prepare the pilaf mix as instructed, but fifteen minutes before it is ready begin to add the ingredients in the order listed. The curry powder must be added first and mixed in well. Then stir in each of the vegetables you have aboard, one after another, and simmer. Do not add the cheese until the last five minutes and then stir it into the hot mixture well. You may need to cook the entire mixture a bit longer than recommended by the mix; if so add about $\frac{1}{4}$ cup of water for each additional five minutes. Serve hot with slices of pita bread on the side.

Starboard Tack, Portside Galley Sandwiches
(created by Peter Fifield)

Use good bread. I use two 6-inch whole wheat pita loaves or two slices of "When Pigs Fly Six Grain & Pumpkin Seed" bread. Add a quarter pound of quality turkey or roast beef, deli-style mustard, hot peppers, sliced dill pickles, and a good deal of romaine lettuce. My most recent addition is ripe avocado spread on one side.

Poached Catch of the Day
(created by Peter Fifield)

Fresh fish just carried from the dock
Orange juice and wine
Grated ginger

Put the fish and liquid in a skillet and simmer covered until the fish flakes with a fork. It could not be simpler or more delicious. Serve with salad, pilaf, or both.

18

The LONDON Trade: Total Boat Cost 1998–2002

LONDON and I are in a cycle of sailing and restoration. In the cold months, while she sits on her stands, I repair what is broken and then make improvements. In the warm months I always seem to launch her with the intention of making a few more changes once she is in the water. These modifications rarely get done. It is always easier to cast off and go sailing, saying, "I will fix that later."

At times LONDON has looked like the classic yacht I know she is; at other times, like any middle-aged creature of the deep, she shows her age, her wrinkles and blemishes. Not surprising considering she endures constant changes, always making a transition to a new sail, a new hull color, a new dodger. And because I am always working on her, I am also very nearly always spending money on her.

I have kept all my receipts. After four-plus years of tinkering with LONDON's equipment, and wandering the aisles and perusing the catalogs of marine stores, I know the cost. And I am rather proud of it.

My boating economy is the moderate expenditure of a land resident and a coastal sailor. I make my living ashore and plan to continue doing so. I have kids in college and a business to run. I have no plans to set sail for the South Seas, and so there is no immediate requirement to stretch out my nest egg to increase the number of days I can remain at sea. There are a number of wonderful books written about that approach to cruising, but this is not one of them.

My boating economy is built on three principles. The first is to enjoy sailing with moderate expenditure. I think I have succeeded. At the same time, I want a boat that is well and safely equipped, and if a new halogen reading light for my berth takes my fancy, I want to be able to buy it. The second is to enjoy my sailing time without going into debt. I pay my expenses in cash. No loans are involved. The third is that the sailing expenditure must be in balance with the whole of our domestic spending. Sailing is a big part of our lives, but it is not everything. We still want to travel, eat out, fix the house, educate our children, etc.

My dream of owning a sailboat was made possible by a single cash windfall of $10,000. Once that money was available for a boat purchase, all the incremental expenses were easy.

Here are the total expenditures divided by calendar year, rather than boating season.

1998	12,049.32
1999	7,836.12
2000	7,437.19
2001	6,903.89
2002	4,168.29
Grand Total	$38,394.81

The grand total includes the 27-foot Cape Dory sailboat, hard and inflatable dinghies, a 5 hp four-cycle outboard engine, a seasonal mooring, boat storage and transport, maintenance, insurance, and all parts and accessories. These numbers also include all shipping and taxes.

The total of $38,400 includes two types of expenditure: asset purchases and ongoing expenses. For my purposes here, assets are the things we could resell for cash. Even being conservative, I think we can say LONDON and the dinghies would fetch $22,000 if I chose to sell them. This leaves some $16,400 as the unrecoverable cash expense of four years of sailing. And this tells me:

$16,400/four years = $4,100 cost per year.

Not too bad. Think of how much it costs to play golf, or what the health-swim-tennis club membership goes for. As I tell my wife, who seems to be the one to whom I am always explaining how little all this is costing, some of the powerboats zooming by us must spend this much each year just on fuel!

And, if we push on into really creative accounting, and subtract the $10,000 windfall as money that was going to be spent anyway, or as money that never really existed—because it was never earned—why, then we are hardly spending money at all: $6,400 over four years.

There has also been some associated income, from my writing about sailing and boat restoration. I estimate it at $2,800 over the four-plus years. Once this is subtracted, we arrive at $3,600 over four years: a mere $900 per year. We are very close to making money. I can't think of another activity where I could be spending this much money while actually only losing $900 a year.

Here are the details of the year by year expense.

1998	Item	$ Price	Comments
9/25/98	Engine inspection	100.00	Pre-closing
9/30/98	Cape Dory 27	10,500.00	1977 CD27, hull No. 35
10/9/98	Boat survey	425.00	Giffy Full & Associates
10/12/98	C.M. Transport	325.00	Move to house
10/23/98	West Marine: Cetol, grease	75.41	
11/23/98	Spartan Marine: parts,	52.32	Bronze vent, grease
12/16/98	Defender: plumbing (DF)	390.18	
12/18/98	West Marine: plumbing	79.38	
12/31/98	West Marine: plumbing	102.03	
1998	**Total**	**12,049.32**	

In the first year, 1998, I had just taken possession of LONDON and the things I bought came straight off the list of immediately needed repairs. These included cleaning supplies, grease, all kinds of hoses and clamps, valves and vents—for drains, for fresh water, for engine cooling, for waste. Epoxy and seacocks. I went through $12,050 in four months. This would be the most rapid period of spending.

1999	Item	$ Price	Comments
01/13/99	WM: plumbing	35.82	
01/15/99	Sailrite (SR): halyards	219.08	Replacing wire with rope
01/18/99	WM: plumbing	109.25	
01/28/99	WM: parts	166.84	
02/08/99	UK Sails: repair	158.90	Genoa repair
02/10/99	WM: parts	37.41	
03/02/99	DF: life jackets and parts	483.74	Safety equipment
03/07/99	Earls Marina (ER): mooring	729.00	LONDON's first mooring
03/07/99	ER: mooring pendant	100.00	New pendant
03/20/99	WM: fiberglass, paint, batteries	397.09	
04/22/99	WM: parts, wire	97.74	
05/02/99	WM: parts, wire	136.54	
05/05/99	WM: fuel tank	157.99	New fuel tank
05/06/99	BoatU.S. (BU): electrical parts, flares	68.79	
05/08/99	BU: shackle, blocks, etc.	129.66	
05/12/99	WM: parts	12.09	
05/18/99	C.M. Transport	341.50	LONDON's launch!
05/23/99	WM: parts	27.56	
05/26/99	DF: barometer, rope	110.00	
05/26/99	WM: line	34.15	
05/28/99	WM: parts	71.80	
05/28/99	Hard dinghy	850.49	Named IMP

06/08/99	DF: dish rack, lights	113.40	
06/14/99	WM: Autohelm ST2000+	625.00	New auto-tiller
07/08/99	WM: Origo stove, inverter	435.44	
09/30/99	ER: mooring	765.45	For 2000 season
10/09/99	BU: parts	46.68	
10/30/99	C.M. Transport	480.50	LONDON hauled out
12/14/99	WM: parts	25.67	
12/29/99	MC: CQR, etc.	237.54	
12/30/99	BU: electrical parts	73.00	
	Insurance	558.00	
1999	**TOTAL**	**7,836.12**	

In 1999 I built up to a crescendo of spending that ran right through July 8, when I replaced the old pressurized alcohol stove with a new non-pressurized one. I had simply had it with spending half an hour coaxing the stove into life. A few weeks before I had bought a new auto-tiller. These two purchases, while both useful and successful, accounted for more than $1,000 of expense.

All the additions after May 18 were done on the water, either at the docks in Quincy or later on the mooring at Fairhaven, where LONDON lay from about the beginning of June. It was during this time that I bought a new hard dinghy and oars in Hingham, a new barometer, a teak dish rack for the cabin, and an inverter to provide 120-volt power off the batteries. I was moving into my new floating home and decorating, seeing what I needed. After the stove purchase in early July, spending suddenly stopped. I wonder if Nancy said something. In any case, I was set for the remainder of the summer. The engine was by now running reliably and I went sailing. In the fall of 1999 I began to stock up for the next winter's projects and improvements.

2000	Item	$ Price	Comments
01/02/00	DF: traveler	311.02	
01/09/00	SR: dodger kit, riding sail, line	401.52	
02/16/00	Consumers Marine Electronics: handheld VHF radio, meter, etc.	249.59	
03/09/00	Marine Exchange (ME): lifelines	122.01	
03/10/00	Excise tax	70.00	
03/20/00	DF: GPS, CQR bow roller, radar reflector	226.33	
04/17/00	ME: roller-furler and headstay	881.00	
04/18/00	SR: luff conversion kit	111.68	For new furler
05/09/00	WM: Reef hook, line, etc.	76.71	
05/11/00	C.M. Transport	350.00	Haul and launch
06/16/00	DF: Zodiac and motor	2,627.05	Inflatable dinghy
06/21/00	Mystic Scenic Studios: LONDON 's lettering	183.75	
06/22/00	WM: inflatable parts	59.29	
06/22/00	WM: inflatable registration	30.00	
07/25/00	Monahan's Marine: inflatable oar	58.64	Lost a Zodiac oar
08/19/00	BU: binoculars, stove fuel	74.83	
08/22/00	WM: flags	35.83	
09/11/00	SR: Sail repair materials	47.84	
11/01/00	ER: transport	590.10	LONDON hauled out
11/01/00	ER: mooring deposit	300.00	For 2001 season
	Insurance	630.00	Dinghy and boat
2000	**TOTAL**	**7,437.19**	

The year 2000, the millennium, was celebrated in style on LONDON's decks and below. This was a period of prosperity, near the height of our economic bubble, and LONDON reaped some of the rewards: a new roller-furler, a dodger, an inflatable tender with an outboard, a handheld VHF, a fixed GPS receiver, and a traveler all were purchased and put into immediate service.

2001	Item	$ Price	Comments
02/07/01	Doyle Sails: mainsail	1,193.50	Replace mainsail
02/14/01	ER: mooring balance	550.50	For 2001 season
03/21/01	Excise tax	70.00	
03/23/01	WM: depth finder, lights	319.66	
03/27/01	SailNet: gasket	13.23	To fix leaky hatch
03/31/01	ME: backstay, anchor chain	209.24	
04/01/01	Mooring sticker	10.00	
04/03/01	HV: outboard tune-up	103.50	
04/04/01	Cape Dory Association membership	40.00	
04/05/01	BU: sail cover, tools	251.05	
05/08/01	BU:	88.15	
05/13/01	ER: transport	470.00	LONDON's launch
05/13/01	ER: cutless bearing, shaft, labor	1,228.40	Resulted in a dry boat
05/29/01	BU: boathook, block, etc.	38.16	
07/22/01	ER: engine work	87.50	
08/24/01	Bluewater Books and Charts: charts	71.35	
08/24/01	WM: Lifevest, strobe, etc.	210.67	
08/25/01	ER: dinghy wash	15.00	
08/27/01	Boxell's Chandlery: charts	39.00	
09/13/01	Portland Yacht Services (PYS): haul	334.50	LONDON hauled out

09/21/01	PYS: engine repair	225.98	To fix oil seal
10/29/01	ER: mooring deposit	300.00	For 2002 season
11/27/01	PYS: balance	334.50	Winter storage in Maine
12/19/01	Excise tax	70.00	
	Insurance	630.00	Dinghy and boat
2001	**TOTAL**	**6,903.89**	

In 2001 a number of maintenance items caught up with us. I replaced the twice-torn mainsail, an errant depth finder, a backstay, and a trashed cutless bearing. These replacements and the repair of an engine oil leak, eventually resolved in Portland, Maine, accounted for half of the year's expenditures. Once they were complete LONDON was a much more impressive and a drier boat.

2002	Item	$ Price	Comments
02/12/02	ER: mooring balance	607.20	For 2002 season
03/10/02	Excise tax	70.00	
04/09/02	Mass. dinghy registration	30.00	
04/26/02	Aqua City: water filter	32.95	
06/01/02	Mooring sticker	10.00	Fairhaven, Mass.
08/06/02	PYS: launch, engine work	623.37	Engine service and launch on 6/22/02
08/22/02	WM: parts	22.82	
09/14/02	BU: coax	1.05	
10/17/02	ER: mooring deposit	350.00	For 2003 season
10/25/02	Harding Sails (HS): new genoa (120%)	550.00	Deposit
11/12/02	ER: haul	639.30	LONDON hauled out
11/21/02	HS: new genoa	601.60	Received sail
	Insurance	630.00	Dinghy and boat
2002	**TOTAL**	**4,168.29**	

The original genoa would begin to shred along the leech late in the season. I kept it in service from late in August until the middle of November through judicious and generous applications of sail repair tape (purchased August 22) and frequent use of the working jib. The new 120% genoa I had made locally accounts for one quarter of the 2002 expenditure.

19

LONDON's Library Reviewed

LONDON was refloated on a sea of books. In his autobiography, Arthur Ransome, the author of *We Didn't Mean to Go to Sea*, describes his first job in London working as a publisher's assistant. One of his tasks was to deliver packages of books. In this way he came to know his way around the city, which he said "was marked for me by bookshops as the sea is marked by buoys[23]."

In an analogous way books have guided me through LONDON's restoration. They inspire my sailing and satisfy a curiosity about the nature of sea life. I would like to recommend some of the books that have been important during the annual cycles of refurbishing and then sailing along the New England coast.

Rich gave me a copy of *Sensible Cruising: The Thoreau Approach* at about the time we began sailing cruising boats, when he and I were members of the Boston Harbor Sailing Club—known to us as "The Club." We took courses there for our sailing certifications. We began by sailing Soling keelboats and ended by taking a full-sized sailboat on an overnight cruise. The on-the-water classes were supplemented by a series of evening lectures on topics such as weather and diesel engine maintenance. After reaching a certain proficiency, you could also arrange to use one of the club boats. The fleet ranged from many Solings and Pearson 26s up to a pair of 39-foot Cals. We spent years hanging around the club buying various memberships and taking more classes, but mostly we sailed in and around Boston Harbor.

Ironically we joined the Club right after we each had received a certificate for bareboat sailing. Over the course of a week in the Florida Keys, Rich, his wife Peggy, Nancy, and I all went on a "Learn to Sail" cruise. We left from midway down the Keys and sailed to Key West and back. It was one of our best vacations, but after it was over we didn't yet feel we were completely proficient cruisers—hence The Club.

The boat we sailed in Florida was a 39-foot fiberglass sloop with a center cockpit and an aft cabin. Peg and Rich took the aft cabin, Nancy and I the forward V-berth, and Captain Joe slept amidships. Captain Joe, our instructor for the week, was a former pharmaceutical salesman from the Midwest. He had adopted the Keys look, loose and cool, tan and a little shaggy. Joe lived with his girlfriend on a small sailboat tied to a wall near the marina. Joe quoted Jimmy Buffett to us as he showed us the ropes, around the boat and around the Keys.

> It's those changes in latitudes, changes in attitudes
> Nothing remains quite the same[24].

We could not have had a better captain for absorbing the Keys ambience. The first day we met Joe at the boat late in the afternoon. He let us aboard and got us settled in, showing us linens and hatches, how to use the stove, and where the drinks were. We would sleep on the boat for the remainder of the trip. Joe would sometimes sleep with us and sometimes sleep ashore. This was a weekly routine for him. Sunday night at Marathon, Tuesday near Little Pine Key, Wednesday night in Key West, and so on. An awesome routine of regular relaxation. On the first day we did one maneuver with the boat and only one: We backed the boat out of the slip and then pulled her straight back in. After that Joe left us on our own. He went back to his own boat to sleep and returned in the morning.

The next morning we repeated our leaving-the-slip maneuver and then, beaming with pride, set off for Hawk Channel, got our sails up, and flew downwind. By 2:00 P.M. we had the anchor down in the mangrove swamp that was the day's destination. Joe settled in for a long afternoon nap. We sat around. We waited for him to wake. There was no dinghy; we were confined to the boat.

When he awoke things livened up. We laughed and drank beer and wine. We ate, we talked. We were sailors now and free of the irritations of land, relishing the life in the turquoise water. We began to hear the refrain of Captain Joe's expressions. With these words he cast off all ties to a life of hassle, a life of land-borne acquisitive stress. One of his expressions—"That's why I sail"— would become one of our own.

During the entire week I only once saw Joe stress. It was right after we'd left Key West. Key West was the jewel in the schedule. Joe had thoroughly regaled us with tales of the crews he'd taken there. There were the four European stewardesses who wanted to sail naked—that was fine with Joe. On another trip, the wife had hosed the vomit off her drunken husband, who lay facedown on the dock in Key West. Once she had him cleaned off, she turned off the hose, curled it up neatly on the dock, and climbed back into her bunk, leaving him sprawled on the dock. There were tales of the antics of the daughter from hell and the crew that never returned to the boat—all the characters Joe had lived with for a week and taught to sail to this fingertip of America.

However, Captain Joe had a real thing about provisioning. We spent more time talking about how to provision than on any other aspect of sailing. When he sent us to the supermarket, he told us over and over again to stay together.

It was a little surreal. We were under his spell. We listened intently as he described how to count how many meals we were buying and how to organize the grocery list he would send us to the store with. He tapped the list with his finger and looked us in the eye. We must stay together. If we did not stay together, we would not be sure we had found everything on the list. He'd seen it happen again and again. We would get out to sea and there would be no chicken.

The test finally came. We were going solo—food shopping. He released us with a parting cry of "Stay together!" I am sure he watched us make our way down the dock, stopping to look over every boat, and then head off into Key West. Joe settled down on the boat for an afternoon nap. The four of us got to the market and split up.

Sailing across Hawk Channel later that afternoon, way out near the reef and well away from land, Joe discovered we had forgotten the Triscuits.

"Did you stay together?" he demanded. One by one we lied to him. Of course we had stayed together. After all, he was the captain.

This introduction to the cruising life made us sailors. Not in the sense that we were suddenly skilled, but rather that we now thought about sailing and boats a lot. Which brings us back to the book at hand, *Sensible Cruising*. The book contains plenty of practical cruising information, but what makes it unique is the way it develops an attitude toward sailing and cruising. An attitude that is different from Captain Joe's laid-back goals, but one he would have been comfortable with. *Sensible Cruising*, by Don Casey and Lew Hackler, is a study in how to acquire a boat you can afford and make the most of it immediately. Go cruising! it cries, using the "Thoreau Approach."

The cruising guide is modeled on Thoreau's classic work, *Walden*. For us this was appropriate in several ways. First Thoreau is our native son: Walden Pond is perhaps 5 miles from my house and even closer to Rich's. The site of Thoreau's father's pencil mill is a 2.5-mile walk into the woods from my back door. We walk the same woods Henry David did. Second, there is a strong emphasis on economy throughout the book. For instance:

> His [Thoreau's] commitment to thrift makes him an authority on "sensible cruising." . . . Thoreau in a very real sense tells us if cruising is what we want, then it is what we should be doing. Take the boat you already have and go[25].

Early on the authors dismiss the necessity of buying that big cruising boat. One section is titled "The 40-Foot Myth"; another "The Sensible Boat."

This book, like Captain Joe, had a seminal influence on my ideas about cruising in a sailboat. I heard a familiar voice. *Sensible Cruising* is inspirational, practical, and I highly recommend it.

I began to discover and read the literature of boat repair and refurbishing. Don Casey has a number of books, including the very useful *This Old Boat,* which focuses on finding and fixing up a run-down fiberglass boat. This book and *Spurr's Boatbook: Upgrading the Cruising Sailboat* were my constant companions when I was beginning to work on LONDON. In particular, I was inspired by some of the projects illustrated in *Spurr's Boatbook,* in which Daniel Spurr rebuilds a Pearson Triton. The Triton was designed by Carl Alberg and is similar in size and form to a Cape Dory 27. (The Triton is 17 inches longer overall, 8 inches longer on the waterline, and 2 inches narrower at maximum beam, and it has the same draft. The Triton is not as bowed out amidships as much as my Cape Dory, but maintains her width over more of her length.) The illustrations in *Spurr's Boatbook* are exceptional and animated by cats.

Here I found the galley foot pump (Figure 5-19) I would install in LONDON. Pressurized water was out for me, since some members of my family come from those places to the south where they leave the water running while washing the dishes. The foot pump makes this impossible and has kept LONDON's water tank full and the captain and crew at peace. A happy ship, thanks to a pump.

Spurr's Boatbook was also an excellent overview to the systems of a boat and enormously useful when I was in the stage of identifying the various parts and what they did. The very first chapter, titled "The Anatomy of a Cruising Sailboat," is a terrific overview of the benefits and trade-offs inherent in different boat designs. And it was great to find John Masefield again, quoted on the first page: "And all I ask is a tall ship and a star to steer her by."

The other book I relied on during the rebuild process was Nigel Calder's *Boatowner's Mechanical and Electrical Manual.* This dense and authoritative work was useful during the restoration and after. Here I found the answer to my mechanical inquisition, how to bleed a diesel engine. Calder's detailed discussion of various roller-furlers and how they work helped me understand why the original unit I had on LONDON was failing. Finally, the sections on electronics and how to diagnose electrical problems guided me in testing and refurbishing my own circuits.

About a year ago, my wife left her job in the software industry and took a new one working for a major supplier of marine electronics. One cold evening while I was home in Massachusetts poking through the refrigerator looking for some poor morsels of food, she called from the sunny boat show she was attending in Annapolis. She began to describe her dinner the night before.

"We had a great time last night at dinner. I met a very funny guy you would just love. He's kind of technical and so nice. He's a writer. He met his wife when he sailed her across the channel from England to Holland. You would really get along with him. Nigel is . . ."

"You had dinner with Nigel Calder?"

"Yeah, that's his name. Have you heard of him?"

It wasn't fair. Her new job should have been my job. She hadn't shown much interest when I was obsessed with seacocks and bilge pumps and would talk about them from dawn to dusk. I could have talked to Nigel about these things—for a very long time.

Only a month before Nancy had been at a press event for the start of the "Around Alone" solo sailing race and had been introduced to Sir Robin Knox-Johnston. Not surprisingly, she seemed somewhat at a loss as to who he was.

"You met Knox-Johnston? I can't believe it! I am just reading about him. In that book I showed you, *A Voyage for Madmen*. What's he like? Do you remember that sailboat we saw in the lobby of the Maritime Museum in Greenwich? That's his boat! He sailed around the world alone in that."

Knox-Johnston and the other sailors who have written and been written about offer a literature of heroic legends to inspire us. I don't know how many descriptions I've read about rounding Cape Horn. You could probably compile a good-sized book just on this topic—there are so many stories, from Joshua Slocum to Bill Tilman, Moitessier, and Chichester—each is unique, each is exciting, and I must have read most of them. The bold chronicles of the ocean voyager are a constant reminder of greater challenges that taunt and tease coastal sailors like myself. Yet when I opened L. Francis Herreshoff's book *Sensible Cruising Designs* and read his statement, "I have never made any long ocean voyages in small craft or had the least desire to do so, preferring rather to anchor each night in a well-sheltered cove," I felt a kind of relief. It is okay to be coastal. Herreshoff said so.

For the enthusiast of the well-developed keel, Herreshoff's book is a delight. Where else can you slip your eyes across so many full-keeled forms? *Sensible Cruising Designs* is filled with beautiful writing, detailed plans and construction notes for nine of his designs, and a portfolio of another forty-six sailing craft of all sizes.

Another book about marine architecture I found engaging was the textbook *Understanding Boat Design* by Brewer and Betts, an introduction to the concepts and thinking of the yacht designer. The section "Language of the Naval Architect" defines the terms the naval architect uses—Prismatic Coefficient, Moment to Trim, Center of Buoyancy, and the like. Numerous sketches illustrate hull shapes, waterline shapes, buttock types, keel profiles, sheerlines, rigs, and bow shapes. A final yacht design book I would recommend is William Atkin's *Of Yachts and Men*, a narrative account of his years designing small boats and sailing them on local waters.

Once you have discovered that you can afford a boat, read some inspiring sailing adventures, and studied boat form, it is time to learn how to sail and navigate and all that. Although we took classes on the water, there were still times when I needed to refer to a book to re-learn the parts of a sail—Is that the luff or the leech?—or check that the pattern of lights seen up ahead is not a barge under tow. The clear leader for me among the learn-to-sail books is *The Annapolis Book of Seamanship* by John Rousmaniere. It covers the basics and presents them with plenty of clear illustrations that clarify the physics of pushing a boat across the water with the wind. This is one of the books I keep on the boat in the summer. My copy has suffered from the damp and from being jammed in that narrow locker behind the seat back. I don't think it left the locker last year, but I like to know it is there. It has a new companion in that dark space, *Nigel Calder's Cruising Handbook*, a detailed and technical book where you can find tables with titles like "Modified Working Load Limits for Anchor Rodes." This is a heavy book packed with data-system troubleshooting advice.

Other books I take sailing with me are the cruising guides, the field guides, and *Eldridge*. *Eldridge Tide and Pilot Book* is unique to the East Coast—a kind of *Old Farmer's Almanac* for Yankee sailors. This famous yellow periodical, which has been published annually for more than 120 years, contains tide and current information for the coast from Florida to Nova Scotia. It lists the tides and currents, sunrises and sunsets, phases of the moon, and all the other almanac information you would expect. It is required reading for the Massachusetts coastal sailor: The tidal current charts for Buzzards Bay and Vineyard and Nantucket Sounds make up the core of the book. It also contains sections on Emergency First Aid, Rules and Regulations, Lights and Fog Signals, Flags and Codes, Astronomical Data, Distress Calls, Coast Guard Stations, Weather Data, and nautical advice and lore. The book runs about 270 pages. I keep my old ones so that later when I need to check from some note in my log what the tide was doing at a particular time, it is an easy exercise.

I keep three cruising guides aboard. For local use I rely on the thorough *Cruising Guide to Narragansett Bay and the South Coast of Massachusetts*. I also carry the classic *Cruising Guide to the New England Coast*, but my favorite read is the *Cruising Guide to the Coast of Maine*, published by Diamond Pass Press. This is the model cruising guide. Do not sail to Maine without buying this book the winter before. My edition describes 530 harbors, but they seem endless and endlessly enticing. Many harbor descriptions include small sketch-charts to orient you to features described in the text. My copy is tattered and worn; there is a piece of small line still marking the pages for Kittery, where I hoped to stop on my last trip down from Portland. At 462 pages, the book offers many illustrations and sketch-charts. It also features an easy-to-use harbor rating system for Protection,

Beauty and Interest, and Facilities, as well as sidebar articles on Maine history and lore. The publisher maintains a very informative website (http://www.diamondpass.com/).

Diamond Pass Press is named after the narrow passage that runs between Peaks Island and the Diamond Islands in Casco Bay. I have not visited the company's office on Peaks Island, although Nancy and I were invited to spend a weekend in a cottage on Peaks that had been rented by our friends Pete and Sandy. It was just after moving LONDON south for the season and my arm was still in a sling, so scrambling around on the rocks had to be done carefully. Also there for the weekend were John and Louise and most of our kids. Peaks is a wonderful place. It is just a quick ferry ride from downtown Portland and yet quiet and somewhat wild. The view from the cottage was so stunning that much of the time we sat on the porch in swings and rockers looking out to sea at the same water I'd sailed across a week before when sailing LONDON from Portland to Fairhaven.

On that trip I had not been sailing solo but I often do, so I have read another pile of books on single-handed sailing. Among them a few stand out. Tristan Jones's *One Hand for Yourself, One for the Ship* is full of fierce opinion and practical ideas on coping at sea alone, including how to stay alive, eat well, and coexist with the locals in third-world ports. He writes:

> I sometimes get the impression that landlubbers look upon voyagers, especially single-handers, as philistines interested in nothing but back-splices and beer. This is simply not so. Alcard, Bardieaux, Moitessier, Tangvald—all these and many more could discuss any aspect of art for hours on end. I never met a true voyager who did not appreciate art in all its forms.

Tristan anticipates situations in order to stay out of trouble. If you don't, it is easy to get into situations where two hands are just not enough.

Another book in this genre is Frank Mulville's *Single-Handed Sailing*. This book focuses on the art and the philosophy of sailing alone.

It includes a number of practical tips from the author's own experiences on how to manage various situations under sail and in harbor, but is most interesting in its unique discussions of the single-hander's mental attitudes, habits, aims, and mental pitfalls. One of my favorite bits comes from the chapter titled "Trials of the Man Alone" in the section "Hypnosis of Solitude":

> The imagination runs riot when a man is alone. Ideas grow explosively in the sub-conscious, feeding themselves on solitude and swelling until they fill the spaces of the mind, pushing out all rational thought and making it difficult to form sensible judgements—an intellectual intoxication.

There are certain works of fiction, like certain sailing trips, in which mental intoxication is essential to the general purpose, the apparent story, the foreseeable pleasure of the thing. Melville's *Moby Dick* and Poe's *The Narrative of Arthur Gordon Pym* spring to mind. Recently I read another book that inspired me to insular adventure, *Hippolyte's Island* by Barbara Hodgson. The hero of this novel, an explorer named Hippolyte, sets out to rediscover a group of lost islands from the deck of his sailboat SOUTHERN SARACEN. The book is filled with richly detailed color illustrations, maps, and journal illustrations of flora, fauna, and geographical features from the imaginary islands, called the Auroras. Here is one passage:

> He reached out and sorted through the maps on the floor, grabbing the three that identified the Auroras. Questions raced through his mind as he studied the aged paper, engraved lines and elegant lettering. If the Auroras did exist, then why had they been dropped off of some maps? If they didn't exist, why were they on these? Who found them? Who lost them[26]?

A premise of this novel is that, in unlikely corners of the world, certain islands have vanished from the maps, from the very geographic consciousness of their region, and remain shrouded in mystery. Hippolyte sets out to find one of these island groups off the coast of South America and then write a book about it, although his adventure of discovery begins by learning to sail.

In *The Voyage of the NARWHAL*, Andrea Barrett combines the wonder of scientific discovery with a captivating adventure set in the age of classification. In 1855 Erasmus Darwin Wells joins an expedition of discovery to the Arctic. This is a narrative of physical struggle, love and jealousy, arrogance and fame. Rich in the lore of nineteenth-century science, this wonderful story is illustrated with copies of engravings from period books. The book opens with Erasmus on the deck of the NARWHAL preparing for departure, loading supplies, but looking over the side into the water between the ship and the wharf:

> He saw, beneath the transparent shadow, what his father had taught him to see: the schools of minnows, the eels and the algae, the mussels burrowing into the silt; the diatoms and the desmids and the insect larvae sweeping past hydrozoans and infant snails. *The oyster,* his father once said, *is impregnated by the dew; the pregnant shells give birth to pearls conceived from the sky. If the dew is pure, the pearls are brilliant; if cloudy, the pearls are dull . . .*

This last thought reminds me: The wonder, the beauty, the health of the sea we sail over is paramount. The sea is not simply there to provide a slippery surface to slide our boats over; it is a living organism. I think of the sea as a living fluid, a kind of culture medium in which life is supported and nurtured, encouraged into variation and abundance.

At the extremes of oceanic description are the two science books I return to again and again. The first is the Smithsonian's *SeaLife: A Complete Guide to the Marine Environment*. This is a massive, all-encompassing work about all of the world's oceans—their physical and biological nature. From the detailed anatomical drawing of a shark's hearing organs, to thermoclines, gyres, and the history of oceanography, it is all here, with a complete field guide to the life in and above the sea. This is a book for a lifetime of browsing.

The second is the very different *Ecology of Buzzards Bay: An Estuarine Profile*. This report discusses the ecosystem of Buzzards Bay, especially in the context of its greater watershed. While it is encouraging to read that "Buzzards Bay remains one of the few relatively pristine bays in the metropolitan corridor from Washington to Boston," the report also makes it clear that parts of the bay have been degraded and others are threatened. This report is fairly technical in places, but a general reader can get a real sense of the interactions at play in the life of the bay. From this book I gained a richer perspective on LONDON's home waters.

We are what we sail. We are what we float upon. I see these books as Ransome saw his London bookshops: buoys marking a voyage of learning across a sea that grows richer and more varied while we make our passage.

20

LONDON Online

It is hard to overstate how much I relied on the Internet in the process of getting LONDON back in the water and even in sailing her. Below I describe the ways I used the Internet during this project and discuss some of the websites I use. I intend no endorsement of one website over another. The sites mentioned are simply those I have become familiar with. There are plenty of alternatives.

There is no Internet connection on LONDON herself and I doubt there ever will be. Once on the boat we like to relax and keep things simple, and getting away from the wonderful information monster is one way to do so.

LONDON's Website

I started photographing LONDON as soon as I got her home. Since I work for a company that does web-based publishing, and I spend a good part of my working days writing HTML, JavaScript, and other web codes, it was easy to post these images to a website. I am not alone. There are scores of well-loved old boats on the Internet, and a number of websites showing the progress of restoration projects. One example is the Boatbuilding Ring, a web ring (a series of linked sites) about boatbuilding, boat design, and restoration (http://www.boatdesign.net/ring/).

Maintaining a website for LONDON has brought me into contact with many other people working on similar projects across the country and has been a continuing source of pride and gratification. Pictures of some of the people and places mentioned in these pages can be found on LONDON's site (http://www.pbaumgartner.com). Some of these photos were the basis of the black and white sketches in this book.

Research

I look for information on the web by using a search engine and then saving the sites I want to go back to in a hierarchy of *favorites* in my browser. My search engine is Google (http://www.google.com). I use Google because it works so well and the initial page is simple and fast.

One of the marine creatures discussed above is the ocean sunfish, *Mola mola*. You might wonder what this strange and ugly fish looks like. Just see what you get if you use Google to do a search for *Mola mola*—it is wonderful. The Internet is loaded with this kind of popular scientific information.

I can search my local library's catalogs online or search across all the other libraries it is affiliated with. I can request books from other libraries, renew books, and search library databases, all from home. This access has vastly increased the number of books I can conveniently find and use, making me—as my wife teases—a "poster boy for the library."

Weather

In several places above I have talked about listening to the weather radio on the boat, but I often use the Internet before I even get on the boat, from home or the office, to find out what conditions are expected over the next few days in the waters I am planning to sail. My favorite site is the Boston-area office of the National Weather Service (http://www.erh.noaa.gov/er/box/). I simply click on the section of an ocean map I am interested in sailing to get the latest marine forecast for that area. Under the *Marine* sidebar heading is a wealth of other marine weather information, including wind forecast maps for the next three days and tidal and wave height information.

The Boston office is part of the Eastern Region of the National Weather Service (http://www.erh.noaa.gov/er/hq/). The National Weather Service is part of NOAA, the National Oceanic and Atmospheric Administration. A quick visit to their home site (http://www.noaa.gov/) gives an awe-inspiring glimpse at the wealth of information of interest to sailors that is online: The main links cover weather, the study and protection of the oceans and coasts, fisheries, climate, satellites, research, and charting and navigation.

An extensive network of stationary buoys, mostly run by NOAA's National Data Buoy Center, collects data across the Atlantic and Pacific Oceans. The master buoy map (http://www.ndbc.noaa.gov/) can be used to review information from buoys across the Northern Hemisphere. Buoys log wind speed and gusts, water temperature, and wave height and period to give a real-time picture of what is happening at that location. Most of them keep this information for the last twenty-four hours, and historical data are also available. The buoy network is a great source of information. There is also a number to call to hear recorded buoy information over the telephone.

When an announcement appeared on my local National Weather Service site for a conference open to the public, I jumped at the chance to attend the Third Southern New England Weather Conference. The agenda included a number of items I was interested in: information on a new satellite given by people from the NASA Goddard Space Flight Center, popular talks by local weather personalities, and in particular a talk titled "Applications of Oceanographic Analyses from Thermal Infrared Satellite Imagery to the Marine Community" by the well-known Jenifer Clark of Jenifer Clark's Gulfstream (http://users.erols.com/gulfstrm/), a private company that forecasts ocean currents around the world. Their forecasts are purchased by ocean yacht racers and other voyagers.

Jenifer described how they use weather satellite information to analyze the currents of the Gulf Stream, the warm current that flows northeast along the eastern coast of the United States. The Gulf Stream is part of a "gyre," a large-scale ocean circulation. The stream is not a monolithic, constant river of water. It wanders and meanders off the coast, and contains within its flow warm and cold eddies. Warm eddies rotate clockwise at speeds of 1 or 2 knots, and tend to drift west-southwest. Cold eddies are mostly found to the south of the stream and rotate in a counter-clockwise direction. Their current flows can be strong. By knowing the position and strength of these variations in the Gulf Stream and navigating among these eddies to take advantage of the favorable currents, a sailor can make a faster and safer passage across the stream.

Gulf Stream predictions are made by looking at ocean buoy data, thermal satellite data (which show the surface temperature of the ocean), and radar data that detail surface height variations—the surface level of warmer water is slightly higher than colder water. Using these sources a skilled oceanographer can create a forecast of the conditions in the Gulf Stream.

Also represented at the weather conference was the Gulf of Maine Ocean Observing System (GoMOOS). The beautifully designed Go-MOOS website (http://www.gomoos.org) consolidates information about the Gulf of Maine—including hourly buoy data, current and biological information, and satellite images—with a variety of users in mind, from commercial mariners to scientists to government agencies. GoMOOS, a nonprofit organization supported by membership dues, describes itself as a "prototype regional, user-driven, coastal ocean observing system."

These sites just begin to describe the wealth of weather information available on the Internet.

Cape Dory and Other Boat Sites

Even before I bought LONDON I found the website devoted to Cape Dory sailboats (http://www.toolworks.com/capedory) hosted by the California Cape Dory Owners Association, which is one of a number of Cape Dory owner associations. Another is the Cape Dory Sailboat Owners Association (CDSOA, http://www.capedory.org/) with its six regional fleets. Nancy and I belong to the CDSOA.

All of these groups share the same discussion forum, The Cape Dory Board (http://www.toolworks.com/capedory/bboard/). This bulletin board is the gem of the site, where Cape Dory owners can "chat" about boating topics and answer each other's questions. It is a great example of what the Internet does so well: building virtual communities of people with a common interest. Where else could I go to find out the weight of my mast or how to loosen a frozen seacock? During LONDON's restoration I made frequent use of this board. At critical junctures in the project I received the help I needed to keep going and to finish. Near the end of the first phase of restoration, there were half a dozen things I still had not figured out, including how to turn off the engine once I got it started. I posted a message and had answers to all my questions in two days. This bulletin board is an incredible knowledge base for Cape Dory owners and another source of Cape Dory pride[27].

Naturally, owners associations exist and online resources are available for boats other than Cape Dorys. The website for *Good Old Boat* magazine (http://www.goodoldboat.com) offers a comprehensive list of links to sailboat owners associations, manufacturers, and individual's websites. For example, under "Pearson" I found nearly fifty links to websites, online discussion groups, newsletters, and individual boatowners associated with Pearson sailboats of various sizes and generations.

21

LONDON's Wake

*I must go down to the seas again, for the call of the running
tide
Is a wild call and a clear call that may not be denied.*
—John Masefield, from the poem "Sea Fever[28]"

An orange winter sun is rising over the treetops to the east, yet the
thermometer seems unable to rise above zero this morning. The activity at the bird feeder drew me into this corner of our house. The
feeder is a clear plastic tube filled with black oilseed, hung three feet
from the window. The birds are desperate for food in the bitter cold.
They ignore me standing in the window and swarm the six silver
perches. I can see perhaps twenty birds jumping and flitting through
the underbrush, or hurtling through the clear cold air for a peck of
seed. Juncos, morning doves, white-throated sparrows, nuthatches,
and the piggy little goldfinches—who hog the perches until knocked
off by an inbound titmouse—they are all here, with a few squirrels
on the ground for good measure.

When the chickadees fly to the feeder they swoop up and down
as if following the rolling surface of an unseen wave—a wave of
cold air on a transparent sea. The closeness of the birds reminds me
how Moitessier developed an affinity for pelagic waterfowl on his
solo sailing voyage, recounted in *The Long Way.* He went around the
world and then halfway around again. He talked with and fed the

frigate birds, nestled gulls in his lap, and became sentimental about his "Fairy Tern": "My Fairy Tern leaves for a moment, then comes back to fly around the boat. She comes back three times, then flies off WNW, to tell me where the Island is[29]."

This corner of the kitchen is the only spot within the house where I can see LONDON hidden behind the garage for the winter. She is up on stands and covered with a tarpaulin. A picture in blue and white: the deep blue of her plastic tarp, the lighter washed blue of the antifouling paint, and the shiny whites of her fiberglass flanks against the clean snow.

A ridgepole runs fore and aft under the plastic tarp. It hangs from wires strung overhead. I made the pole by cutting down a spindly 40-foot birch and trimming its branches off with an axe. The ridgepole lifts the blue plastic to make a tent over her cockpit, steep enough for the snow to slide off. The tarp is pulled down tight against LONDON's flanks. Decrepit bits of line run under her keel through tarp grommets and are snugged up tight.

The snow is deep this winter. Two weeks ago I used the snow blower to clear a path out to the boat. If it will warm up a bit I can get inside the boat and start taking some measurements for this season's projects. Judging by this morning's temperature, that will not be soon.

Yet the orange sun reminds me of being anchored in Kettle Cove on a quiet night last September, watching the sunset. I am standing on LONDON's foredeck. The fiberglass deck is a bright blue and warm underfoot. Overhead, strands of cloud reach across the vast sky to make purple and ruby banks of floating color. Buzzards Bay is quiet and empty of boats. I have the anchorage to myself. I am at one with my boat.

I feel as if the world is mine. LONDON is mine. I know her inside and out. I know her innards better than I know the inside of my own body. I have crawled and strained into the recess of her forepeak, scraped her bilge, and drilled her hull. I have lain atop her engine and strained to reach her cockpit drains, scrubbed the blue deck, sanded the long teak rail inch by inch.

I know her secrets, I know her crevices. There are lengths of hose hidden in the forepeak. A flashlight is wedged behind battery number one. On the cabintop is a crack made by a bolt of lightning. The pin of the forward hinge on the port cockpit locker is steel, not bronze like the others. These bits of knowledge bind me to her. We have become comfortable together. I know that tonight within the shelter of her small cabin I can sleep safe and sound, dry and warm. LONDON and I have come a long way from that backyard in Quincy nearly five years ago to this cove on the western side of Naushon Island on the edges of Buzzards Bay.

It is roughly 10 miles magnetic south from my mooring to Kettle Cove—an easy trip to a fair weather anchorage, a spot to stay when the weather conditions are stable. The protection here is minimal. Even so it is a special place. The isle of Naushon is privately held. Wandering ashore is strictly forbidden. This has kept the island an exclusive enclave. It has also kept it wild. Anchored in the cove, I can

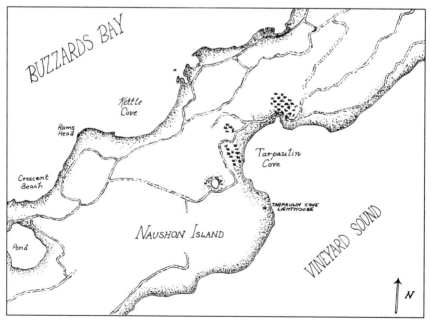

Kettle and Tarpaulin Coves

look at the island, across its meadows, heath, and wood, and see not a single house. Kettle Cove is one of the few places where one is permitted to land on Naushon, along a short stretch of the beach. Access beyond the beach is prohibited. Kettle Cove is directly across the island from the deeper and more protected anchorage at Tarpaulin Cove on the Vineyard Sound side, another favorite spot and one other place where limited beach access is allowed.

When Bartholomew Gosnold first explored these Elizabeth Islands in late May of 1602, he stood on the bluff to the south of this cove and took in the view of Kettle Cove and the mainland beyond. Gosnold began to build a settlement further down the island chain on Cuttyhunk, but decided to return to England three weeks later in his ship CONCORD. He had been unable to muster enough men to stay behind with him[30].

Today Kettle Cove is a place to stop for lunch and a swim, or a walk along the beach, or to anchor on a quiet night and enjoy an unobstructed view of the sunset over Buzzards Bay at the end of the day. After the sun has gone down, other than the distant glow of the lights of New Bedford it is dark here and usually quiet, although I have been woken by schools of fish thrashing the water around the boat into a noisy tempest.

In the morning I've seen young striped bass chasing minnows so far into the shallows that they bounce off the seaweed-covered rocks trying to flee. Sometimes there is a sudden splash and the dripping ascent of an osprey beating hard to lift a fish from the water and carry it off to a treetop on the island.

I think every time I have stopped here, I have swum. The water is warm and clear. I float and swim around the boat, hang from her rails and polish her fiberglass flanks with cool splashes of water. I swim away and look up at her with my face just above the surface. From some angles LONDON appears sublime, from others quite plain.

I like the view of LONDON from astern the best. Her transom has a graceful, lifted shape. Her overhang slaps at the little waves beneath with a lightness, a playful buoyancy I find attractive. As I swim around to be off the stern quarter, she still retains her beauty; her sides appear lengthened toward the bow as if reaching forward.

From abeam she is at her plainest. From the mast aft all seems right, but from the mast forward she seems a little short and squat. Her spoon bow is too close to her mast. From a vantage point off her bow quarter, she again appears to lengthen and reveals some of the sailing grace I know is there. Seen head-on she is a different boat: a big-headed, low-decked force coming right at you.

I swim in to where the anchor line pierces the surface, take three or four deep breaths, and dive under the surface to swim underwater along the rode. I want to see the anchor resting on the bottom.

If I were to sum up the three most important changes I have made to the boat during these cycles of sailing and restoring—beyond all the essential basics that have made the boat easier to sail and cruise—I think I would begin with the anchor. A simple change, but so important. LONDON's main anchor is now a plow-style 25-pound CQR, which I added the second season. The anchor is heavy and awkward, but when it is down I am sure the boat is going to stay put. I had lost that feeling of security for a time after the affair at Lake Tashmoo. I haven't installed the bow roller yet, so I keep the anchor lashed down firmly to the forward deck. A length of the anchor's curved arm wedges in tightly between the rails of the bow pulpit and a deck pipe; then I tie it down at each end.

I have seen two explanations of the name CQR—one an acronym (for "coastal quick release"), the other a mnemonic ("secure"). The latter resonates with me. The phrase "Made in Scotland" is embossed into the metal of the arm.

I have learned to lift the CQR by grabbing it under the curved part of the shaft near the head. I once carried it from the garage out to the boat by holding the very end of the shaft and letting the rest dangle. However, since the plow head is on a pivot and swivels, this is not the way to handle a CQR. While I was walking to the boat, reveling in the manly weight of the thing, the head did swivel and the point of the plow caught the shin bone of my right leg sharply. This spot remained sore for several weeks. I now treat the CQR with respect and carry it more like a cat and less like a sledge hammer. If the anchor is one of the most successful improvements to the boat, mounting the GPS with the other cockpit instruments in the aft bulkhead of the cabinhouse is another. The GPS display is easy to read from the helm and I refer to it constantly. I simply love the information it provides and will not let myself become concerned about my growing dependence upon it. When I am under way, even to somewhere familiar, I will set the GPS to a waypoint ahead. From the display I can see how well I am sailing the boat toward my target. The velocity made good, speed, and estimated time of arrival are all computed and updated. The GPS gives me a speed over the bottom; the knot meter, with its little paddle wheel mounted along the side of the keel, indicates the speed through the water. Assuming everything is calibrated correctly, if the GPS tells me I am sailing at 4 knots and the knot meter tells me I am going at 5, I know I am sailing into 1 knot of opposing current.

Of course, the GPS is most useful in the dark or in fog and haze. In my regular sailing area I have recorded locations I can route myself along and assigned them acronyms. I have accurately plotted these waypoints onto my paper charts. This gives me a private routing system to use when I can't see much further than the bow of the boat, and allows me to make a safe passage well out of the regular (and busy) marked channels. I think one of the worst places to be in the fog is along one of those pre-plotted routes on a nautical chart. Everyone else and his dog are trying to stay on that same line, peering through the gray mist for the next buoy, often moving too fast.

I also carry a spare, handheld GPS and spare batteries for it. If both GPSs failed, do I think I would discover that years of depending on GPS have made my navigational skills atrophy to the point of uselessness? Obviously not. We sailed for many years with a compass and dead reckoning and could do so again. When I hit that rock in Maine, I had the GPS on; I just hadn't bothered to set a waypoint or take another look at the chart. After all, it is not the GPS that will save you; it is being aware of what you are doing, keeping a good watch, and making a note of where you are every half hour.

The third major improvement to LONDON was an effective and reliable mechanical auto-tiller. If I worry about becoming dependent upon any piece of equipment it would not be the GPS, but *auto*. I was born with a map in my head, I can orient myself quickly and reliably, but sometimes when sailing alone I do not have enough hands or a long enough reach to keep her on course and go below. *Auto* frees me to move about the boat. She will not sail herself. She needs a hand, mechanical or human, to keep her in line. She always has a tendency to come up into the wind, a bit of pull on the tiller, especially as the wind picks up. This is okay with me. I like the way she sails and when I have her in hand, cutting across some windy pressure, I know by that pull on the tiller where and how she is moving.

Even with all these improvements, these four seasons of work on her, there are still projects to finish. It seems I can always make her a little better, a little more comfortable, and there is always the ongoing maintenance. This year's project list is fairly long; I didn't do much work on her last winter when she sat in Portland. To keep track of the items, I write them in an inexpensive composition book I use for my logbook and other notes. It is one of the items in the bag that always goes on and off the boat with me.

The first item on the list reads "cockpit hinge"—I broke another hinge. This time I saw it happen: I was getting her wrapped up on a cold day ashore when I stepped on the cockpit locker cover after a piece of ice had fallen into the hinge slot. My weight against the ice forced the cover to lift and snap the pin. I should probably replace the remaining three now.

The roller-furling reefing line cleat needs upgrading. I realized one day when sailing with the big genoa furled that if the roller-furler line let go, the rest of the genoa would roll out in the gusty wind. I would be all the way over. The line runs from the bow through guides and leads along the edge of the deck to a point halfway down the cockpit where a final block turns the line forward again to a plastic cleat. It is just screwed into the cockpit wall. I need to replace this with something more substantial, a metal cleat, bolted through with a backing plate. I have just the piece in the shed. It came off the old mainsheet fastening.

A bow roller for the anchor. I have had this part for two years now. I just have to put it on.

The inner shrouds came unfastened a few times again this year. The problem is the closed-style turnbuckles fastened with nuts on the threaded ends of the shrouds. I would like to replace these with open turnbuckles and cotter pins that can't come undone.

I have bought a new radio to install. The original VHF is beginning to fail. The new one is much smaller and of better quality. I never liked where the radio was placed in the cabin. I will install the new one closer to the companionway so I can reach it from the cockpit when under way.

I want to improve the ventilation in the V-berth and head area. I have been having a slight problem with mildew forming when she's closed up. There are a couple of options for attacking this. I will probably start with a solar-powered exhaust ventilator. LONDON has a traditional-looking teak Dorade box mounted on deck with a white cowl vent above. The Dorade box is also a convenient place to mount an electrical outlet for the forward deck as an alternative spot to plug in the spotlight, or the low-voltage secondary anchor light. I plan to run the wires into the cabin through the existing air passage.

I need a new terminal block for the connections at the base of the mast to the wires for the running, deck, and anchor lights. I have tried several different styles of connectors and they have all corroded after a season or two. I have now found a waterproof model I am hopeful about. I want to replace the existing bow navigation lights with a new set mounted higher, on the bow rail.

The knot meter needs replacement or repair. It worked only intermittently by the end of last season. With the two GPSs I do not strictly need it, but I would feel better if it worked.

Finally, the AM/FM radio in the boat no longer holds onto a signal. It wanders off the station after five or ten minutes and must be manually re-tuned. I have an old car radio I will use as a replacement. I also want to move this radio to a better location or at least make a more attractive flush mount for it.

The new season holds the promise of the cruises not completed last year or the year before. There is always somewhere to reach for. Problems with the depth finder and perhaps end of summer lethargy kept me from completing a sail to Monomoy Island and gunkholing around its shifting shallows. A patch of bad weather kept Rich and me from circumnavigating Cape Cod as we had originally intended. I still have the cruising guide to Nova Scotia, yet have never seen its shores from the sea.

There are also places where I have sailed before, but not in LONDON. I want to take LONDON to some of these old places. I want to go back to Wellfleet, where I spent so many summers, find my way into the harbor, and moor there in the shallow waters off the town pier. We will row ashore and walk beside the narrow road that runs along the edge of the salt marsh, turn to follow other streets up the slight hill into town, and begin a summer evening supper with fresh oysters. It will be dark when we emerge again onto the street satiated and stretch, idly looking in the shop windows, at the inn and the church across the street, and slowly begin to make our way back to the pier. Once back aboard, with the dinghy tied to the stern, we can sit in LONDON's cockpit in the dark and watch couples stroll on the pier from one cone of light to another.

In the morning as we sail away from the town of Wellfleet, after we are out of the narrowest parts of the channel, around the breakwater and in the open part of the harbor, I will hoist the sails. I want to watch LONDON's wake spread the mark of her passage across the salty waters and know that under their surface the oysters are breeding still, healthy and prolific under the wash of the morning tide.

LONDON's Wake

Bibliography

Albion, Robert G. et al. *New England and the Sea* (American Maritime Library, vol. 5). Middletown, Connecticut: Wesleyan University Press, 1972.

Alden, Peter et al. *National Audubon Society Field Guide to New England.* New York: Alfred A. Knopf, 1998.

Atkin, William. *Of Yachts and Men.* Dobbs Ferry, New York: Sheridan House Inc., 1949.

Bailey, Anthony. *The Thousand Dollar Yacht.* Dobbs Ferry, New York: Sheridan House Inc., 1996.

Bailey, Anthony. *The Coast of Summer.* Dobbs Ferry, New York: Sheridan House Inc., 1999.

Barrett, Andrea. *The Voyage of the NARWHAL.* New York: W.W. Norton & Company, 1998.

Beard, Henry and Roy McKie. *Sailing: A Sailor's Dictionary.* New York: Workman Publishing, 1981.

Bickford, Charlene Bangs and Kenneth R. Bowling. *The Birth of the Nation: The First Federal Congress, 1789–1791.* Madison, Wisconsin: Madison House Publishers, 1989.

Bigelow, Henry B. and William C. Schroeder. *Fishes of the Gulf of Maine,* 2nd edition. Washington D.C.: U.S. Fish and Wildlife Service, 1953.

Boschung, Herbert T., Jr. et al. *National Audubon Society Field Guide to North American Fishes, Whales, and Dolphins.* New York: Alfred A. Knopf, 1983, 1997.

Brewer, Edward S. and Jim Betts. *Understanding Boat Design: A Basic Introduction for the Boat Buyer, Amateur Boat Builder, and Beginning Yacht Designer.* Camden, Maine: International Marine, 1972.

Brower, Kenneth. *The Starship and the Canoe.* New York: Harper & Row, Publishers, 1983.

Buckley, William F., Jr. *Airborne: A Sentimental Journey.* Boston: Little, Brown & Co., 1972.

Bull, John and John Farrand, Jr. *National Audubon Society Field Guide to North American Birds.* New York: Alfred A. Knopf, 1977.

Burch, David. *Emergency Navigation: Pathfinding Techniques for the Inquisitive and Prudent Mariner.* Camden, Maine: International Marine, 1986.

Calder, Nigel. *Boatowner's Mechanical and Electrical Manual,* 2nd edition. Camden, Maine: International Marine, 1996.

Calder, Nigel. *Nigel Calder's Cruising Handbook: A Compendium for Coastal and Offshore Sailors.* Camden, Maine: International Marine/ McGraw-Hill, 2001.

Casey, Don. *This Old Boat.* Camden, Maine: International Marine/ Ragged Mountain Press, 1991.

Casey, Don. *Sailboat Refinishing.* Camden, Maine: International Marine, 1996.

Casey, Don and Lew Hackler. *Sensible Cruising: The Thoreau Approach.* Camden, Maine: International Marine, 1986.

Chappelle, Howard I. and Edwin T. Adney. *The Bark Canoes and Skin Boats of North America* (Bulletin 230). Washington D.C.: Smithsonian Institution, 1964.

Chartrand, Mark R. *National Audubon Society Field Guide to the Night Sky.* New York: Alfred A. Knopf, 1991.

Chichester, Sir Francis. *Gipsy Moth Circles the World.* New York: Coward-McCann, Inc., 1967.

Childers, Erskine. *The Riddle of the Sands.* Dobbs Ferry, New York: Sheridan House Inc., 1998.

Childress, Lynda Morris, Patrick Childress, and Tink Martin. *A Cruising Guide to Narragansett Bay and the South Coast of Massachusetts.* Camden, Maine: International Marine, 1996.

Cochrane, Admiral Lord. *The Autobiography of a Seaman.* New York: The Lyons Press, 2000.

Connolly, James B. *The Book of Gloucester Fishermen.* New York: The John Day Company, 1930.

Conrad, Joseph. *The Nigger of the Narcissus: A Tale of the Forecastle.* Garden City, New York: Doubleday, Page & Company, 1914.

Courtauld Institute of Art. *The Courtauld Gallery at Somerset House.* London: Courtauld Institute of Art/Thames and Hudson, Ltd., 1998.

Cramer, Deborah. *Great Waters: An Atlantic Passage.* New York: W.W. Norton & Company, 2001.

Crawford, William P. *Mariner's Weather.* New York: W. W. Norton & Company, 1978.

Cucari, Attilio. *Sailing Ships.* Chicago, New York: Rand McNally & Company, 1976.

Dana, Richard Henry, Jr. *Two Years before the Mast.* New York: Harper and Bros., 1840.

Darwin, Charles. *The Voyage of the BEAGLE,* abridged. New York: Harper & Row, Publishers, 1959.

Dowd, John. *Sea Kayaking: A Manual for Long-distance Touring.* Vancouver: Douglas & McIntyre Ltd., 1986.

Doyle, Sir Arthur Conan. *Complete Sherlock Holmes.* New York: Bantam Doubleday Dell Publishing Group, 1976.

Duncan, Roger F. et al. *A Cruising Guide to the New England Coast.* New York: W.W. Norton & Company, 1995.

Dyson, George. *Baidarka: The Kayak.* Edmonds, Washington: Alaska Northwest Publishing Co., 1986.

Dyson, John. *Yachting the New Zealand Way.* Christchurch, Australia: Whitcombe and Tombs Ltd., 1966.

Edmunds, Arthur. *Fiberglass Boat Survey Manual.* Clinton Corners, New York: John de Graff, 1979.

Eliot, T.S. *Four Quartets.* New York: Harcourt Brace Jovanovich, 1971.

Farson, Robert H. *The Cape Cod Canal.* Middleton, Connecticut: Wesleyan University Press, 1997.

Fleming, Fergus. *Barrow's Boys.* New York: Atlantic Monthly Press, 2000.

Fry, Eric C. *The Complete Book of Knots and Ropework.* Devon, United Kingdom: David & Charles, 1996, 2000.

Garland, Joseph E. *Lone Voyager.* New York: Little, Brown & Co., 1963.

Gessner, David. *Return of the Osprey: A Season of Flight and Wonder.* Chapel Hill, North Carolina: Algonquin Books of Chapel Hill, 2001.

Gibbs, Tony. *Cruising in a Nutshell: The Art and Science of Enjoyable Coastwise Voyaging in Small Auxiliary Yachts.* New York: W.W. Norton & Company, 1983.

Gosner, Kenneth L. *The Atlantic Seashore: A Field Guide to Sponges, Jellyfish, Sea Urchins, and More.* Peterson Field Guides. Boston: Houghton Mifflin, 1978.

Hammick, Anne and Gavin McLaren, editors. *RCC Pilotage Foundation: The Atlantic Crossing Guide,* 4th edition. Camden, Maine: International Marine, 1983, 1998.

Harris, David. *Wreck and Resurrection.* Summerland Key, Florida: Tortuga Books, 2001.

Henderson, Richard. *Sea Sense.* Camden, Maine: International Marine, 1972.

Henderson, Richard. *Singlehanded Sailing,* 2nd edition. Camden, Maine: International Marine, 1988.

Herreshoff, L. Francis. *Sensible Cruising Designs.* Camden, Maine: International Marine, 1973.

Hersey, John. *Blues.* New York: Vintage Books/Random House, 1988.

Hiscock, Eric C. *Cruising under Sail,* 3rd edition. Camden, Maine: International Marine/Ragged Mountain Press, 1986.

Hodgson, Barbara. *Hippolyte's Island.* San Francisco: Chronicle Books, 2001.

Howes, Brian L. and Dale D. Goehringer. *Ecology of Buzzards Bay: An Estuarine Profile.* National Biological Service, Biological Report 31. U.S. Department of the Interior, September 1996.

Jones, Tristan. *One Hand for Yourself, One for the Ship: The Essentials of Single-handed Sailing.* Dobbs Ferry, New York: Sheridan House Inc., 1990.

Jorgensen, Eric. *Sailboat Maintenance.* Arleta, California: Clymer Publications, 1975.

Kales, Emily and David Kales. *All about the Boston Harbor Islands.* Boston: Herman Publishing Inc., 1976.

Kennett, James P. *Marine Geology.* Englewood Cliffs, New Jersey: Prentice Hall, 1982.

Kent, Rockwell. *N by E.* New York: Brewer & Warren, 1930.

Kent, Rockwell. *Voyaging Southward from the Strait of Magellan.* Hanover, New Hampshire: University Press of New England for Wesleyan University, 1999.

Kurlansky, Mark. *Cod: A Biography of the Fish That Changed the World.* New York: Penguin, 1997.

Letcher, John S., Jr. *Self-steering for Sailing Craft.* Camden, Maine: International Marine, 1974.

Maloney, Elbert S. and Charles Frederic Chapman. *Chapman Piloting: Seamanship and Small Boat Handling,* 61st edition. New York: Hearst Marine Books, 1994.

Marryat, Captain Frederick. *Masterman Ready.* London: Thomas Nelson and Sons Ltd. (undated, circa 1959).

Marshall, Roger. *Yacht Design Details.* New York: Hearst Marine Books, 1989.

Masefield, John. *The Poems and Plays of John Masefield: Volume One, Poems.* New York: The Macmillan Company, 1913.

Melville, Herman. *Moby-Dick.* New York: The Modern Library, 2000.

Moitessier, Bernard. *The Long Way.* Dobbs Ferry, New York: Sheridan House Inc., 1995.

Morison, Samuel Eliot. *The Maritime History of Massachusetts,* 1783–1860. Boston: Houghton Mifflin, 1941.

Mulville, Frank. *Single-handed Sailing.* Dobbs Ferry, New York: Sheridan House Inc., 1990.

Mustin, Henry C. *Surveying Fiberglass Sailboats: A Step-by-step Guide for Buyers and Owners.* Camden, Maine: International Marine, 1994.

Neill, Peter, editor. *American Sea Writing: A Literary Anthology.* New York: The Library of America, 2000.

Nichols, Peter. *Sea Change: Alone across the Atlantic in a Wooden Boat.* New York: Penguin, 1997.

Nichols, Peter. *A Voyage for Madmen*. New York: Perennial, Harper-Collins, 2002.

Nicolson, Ian. *Improve Your Own Boat: Projects and Tips for the Practical Boat Builder*. New York: W.W. Norton & Company, 1986.

Nybakken, James W. *Marine Biology: An Ecological Approach*, 2nd edition. New York: Harper & Row, 1988.

Oppel, Frank, editor. *Tales of New England Past*. Secaucus, New Jersey: Castle, 1987.

Pardey, Lin and Larry Pardey. *The Capable Cruiser*. Vista, California: Pardey Books, 1995.

Peffer, Randall S. *Logs of the Dead Pirates Society: A Schooner Adventure around Buzzards Bay*. Dobbs Ferry, New York: Sheridan House Inc., 2000.

Perez-Reverte, Arturo. *The Nautical Chart*. New York: Harcourt, Brace & Co., 2001.

Philbrick, Nathaniel. *In the Heart of the Sea: The Tragedy of the Whaleship ESSEX*. New York: Viking/Penguin Group, 2000.

Ransome, Arthur. *We Didn't Mean to Go to Sea*. London: Jonathan Cape, 1937.

Ransome, Arthur and Rupert Hart-Davis, editor. *The Autobiography of Arthur Ransome*. London: Century Publishing, 1985.

Reid, William James. *The Building of the Cape Cod Canal: 1627 –1914*. Privately printed, 1961.

Reynolds, Sir Joshua. *Discourses on Art*, edited by Robert R. Wark. New Haven: Yale University Press, 1975.

Robbins, Chandler S., Bertel Bruun, and Herbert S. Zim. *Birds of North America: A Guide to Field Identification*. New York: Golden Press/Western Publishing, 1966.

Roberts, John. *Optimize Your Cruising Sailboat: 101 Ways to Make Your Sailboat Better*. Camden, Maine: International Marine, 2000.

Robinson, Nelson B. *The Extraordinary Adventures of Howard Blackburn: Hero Fisherman of Gloucester*, 1978.

Rousmaniere, John. *Fastnet, Force 10*. New York: W.W. Norton & Company, 1980.

Rousmaniere, John. *The Annapolis Book of Seamanship*. New York: Simon & Schuster, 1983.

Schultz, Elizabeth A. *Unpainted to the Last: Moby-Dick and Twentieth-century American Art.* Lawrence, Kansas: University of Kansas Press, 1995.

Severin, Tim. *In Search of Moby Dick: The Quest for the White Whale.* New York: Basic Books/Perseus Books Group, 2000.

Sherwood, Richard M. *A Field Guide to Sailboats*, 2nd edition. Boston: Houghton Mifflin, 1994.

Slocum, Victor. *Capt. Joshua Slocum: The Adventures of America's Best Known Sailor.* Dobbs Ferry, New York: Sheridan House Inc., 1950.

Smith, E. Newbold. *Down Denmark Strait.* Boston: Little, Brown & Co., 1980.

Smith, Robert H. *Smith's Guide to Maritime Museums of North America.* Del Mar, California: C Books, 1993.

Snow, Edward Rowe. *Mysterious Tales of the New England Coast.* New York: Dodd, Mead, 1961.

Sobel, Dava and William J.H. Andrews. *The Illustrated Longitude.* New York: Walker & Co., 1998.

Spurr, Daniel. *Spurr's Boatbook: Upgrading the Cruising Sailboat*, 2nd edition. Camden, Maine: International Marine, 1993.

Stone, Nathaniel. *On the Water: Discovering America in a Rowboat.* New York: Broadway Books, 2002.

Taft, Hank, Jan Taft, and Curtis Rindlaub. *A Cruising Guide to the Maine Coast*, 3rd edition. Peaks Island, Maine: Diamond Pass Press, 1996.

Thaxter, Celia. *Among the Isles of Shoals.* Boston: Houghton Mifflin, 1915.

Theroux, Paul. *Fresh Air Fiend: Travel Writings 1985–2000.* Boston: Houghton Mifflin, 2000.

Tilman, H.W. *The Eight Sailing/Mountain-Exploration Books.* London: Diadem Books Ltd., 1987.

Tirion, Wil. *The Cambridge Star Atlas*, 3rd edition. Cambridge University Press, 2000.

United States Coast Guard Auxiliary. *Sailing and Seamanship*, 4th edition. Washington, D.C.: Coast Guard Auxiliary National Board, 1985.

Upgren, Arthur. *The Turtle and the Stars: Observations of an Earthbound Astronomer.* New York: Times Books/Henry Holt & Co., 2002.

Venn, Tamsin. *Sea Kayaking along the New England Coast.* Boston: Appalachian Mountain Club, 1991.

Vigor, John. *Twenty Small Sailboats to Take You Anywhere.* Arcata, California: Paradise Cay Publications, 1999, 2001.

Walker, Stuart H. *The Sailor's Wind.* New York: W.W. Norton & Company, 1998.

Waller, Geoffrey et al. *SeaLife: A Complete Guide to the Marine Environment.* Washington, D.C.: Smithsonian Institution Press, 1996.

Wardale, Roger. *Nancy Blackett: Under Sail with Arthur Ransome.* London: Jonathan Cape, 1991.

White, E.B. *Essays of E.B. White.* New York: Harper and Row, 1977. (Contains "The Sea and the Wind That Blows.")

White, Marion Jewett. *Eldridge Tide and Pilot Book.* Boston: Marion Jewett White et al., 1999–2002.

Whynott, Douglas. *A Unit of Water, a Unit of Time: Joel White's Last Boat.* New York: Doubleday, 1999.

Wilson, Harold C. *Gosnold's Hope: The Story of Bartholomew Gosnold.* Greensboro, North Carolina: Tudor Publishers, Inc., 2000.

Endnotes

Full references for the books noted here can be found in the Bibliography.

1. *The Starship and the Canoe*, by Ken Brower, is the story of George Dyson's construction of a giant seagoing kayak and his father's research into starships—two vehicles at the extremes of technology. George, who lives alone in a tree house in British Columbia, is looking to the Aleuts for inspiration in his self-propelled craft. His father, the renowned astrophysicist, dreams of building a starship powered by exploding nuclear bombs. The book includes descriptions of kayak voyages along the Inside Passage.

2. *Among the Isles of Shoals* is Celia Thaxter's account of living as the daughter of a lighthouse keeper on White Island. When I opened the book, which was first published in 1873, I expected it would be too pretty or dated; I was wrong. I read it entirely one long, cold January evening near the full moon. Her descriptions of the natural world are beautiful, but I most enjoyed the history and tales of life on the islands and the people who lived there. Her stories range from the prosaic to the supernatural. She wrote the book as one long essay, moving from geographical description of the Isles of Shoals, to the variety of the shoreline, and then the plants, history, and folk ways. A remarkable book.

3. Here is an example of a post I made to the Cape Dory newsgroup (http://www.toolworks.com/capedory/bboard/) on the

morning of November 9, 1998. By the end of the day I had four good responses and was able to proceed with my work.

I have bought a 1977 Cape Dory (#35), which has been out of the water since 1988 and left uncovered and neglected ever since. Think of it as my winter project. I moved the boat alongside my garage, northwest of Boston. Things outside are going well—she's cleaning up real nice.

But as I turn my attention to the systems, and the first is plumbing, I have hit my first problem. All the seacocks are frozen, some open, some shut. Let's take the large one in the head . . . I have removed the nuts and plate (I have a Spartan Marine catalog and other books describing disassembly), used various penetrating oils to loosen the valve, but it will not disassemble. I have tapped it, I have warmed it—okay I even hit it (protected by wood).

So what does one do? Remove it from the boat? If so, is it salvageable? And does anyone have any good ideas about how to get those heavy head hoses off without using a knife?

Thanks for all your help.

Pete

4. For an illustration of an older-style roller-furler, in which the genoa rolls up around a wire luff, see Figure 16-32a in Nigel Calder's *Boatowner's Mechanical and Electrical Manual.*

5. The story of how Joshua Slocum acquired SPRAY is taken from Victor Slocum's biography of his father, *Capt. Joshua Slocum: The Adventures of America's Best Known Sailor* (1950), p. 273.

6. I looked up *Mola mola* in my copy of *Fishes of the Gulf of Maine*, by Bigelow and Schroeder, a second edition published in 1953. This book, which is based mostly on surveys from around the time of WWI, lists the fishes that used to exist in the Gulf of Maine. The authors write: "Our aim is a handbook for the easy identification of the fishes that occur in the Gulf of Maine, with summaries of what is known of the distribution, relative abundance, and more significant facts in the life history of each." The sources of supporting information begin with Captain J. Smith in 1616 and continue up to the work of the authors them-

selves (c. 1950). I think it is unlikely that the fish cataloged still inhabit the Gulf of Maine in anything like the abundance described. I also suspect many are absent entirely. Years ago I met an old fisherman on the town dock in Ipswich where I would often put my kayak in the water. He told me quite simply and brutally through a cloud of tobacco smoke that the fish were all gone in the Gulf of Maine.

However, there is now a third edition of this classic, published by the Smithsonian Press and updated to 2002. A press release about this edition makes me wonder. The first edition was published in 1925 by the Bureau of Fisheries and included 178 fish species in 83 families. The second edition described 219 species in 108 families, while the current edition contains information about 252 species representing 118 families. The release also says:

"Much of the information in the expanded text was derived from bottom-trawl surveys of the Gulf of Maine and adjacent waters conducted every year since the early 1960s by NOAA Fisheries. The editors refer to this survey as 'perhaps the best marine biodiversity database available anywhere.'" (NOAA news release "Classic Marine Fish Guide Revised," NOAA 2002-085, June 27, 2002).

7. For more information about the Shoals Marine Laboratory field station and visiting Appledore Island, see the SML website (http://www.sml.cornell.edu/).

8. Descriptions of Salem in the 1790s are based on Samuel Eliot Morison's *The Maritime History of Massachusetts* (1941), a gem of a book and compelling reading for anyone interested in the history of New England ports and trade. Morison describes the specialties of each coastal town and how they made their profits. In more than a few cases the profits were huge and led to the founding of a number of powerful families. We read letters from a twenty-one-year-old R.B. Forbes trading in France and the West Indies, hear accounts of E.H. Derby fighting his way to the

Mediterranean to trade and sup with Lord Nelson, and learn of Bowditch's life and contributions. Massachusetts is also discussed in the context of the developing nation and world. This book is packed with information and a fascinating read.

9. My remarks on the history of the Cape Cod Canal are based in part on Robert H. Farson's *The Cape Cod Canal* (1997). See also William J. Reid's *The Building of the Cape Cod Canal* (1961) and the government-sponsored report *Ecology of Buzzards Bay: An Estuarine Profile* (1996), pp. 97–98.

10. The allusion for the night's log is *Erebus,* in Greek mythology the god of darkness. Erebus was the offspring of Chaos, the primordial void. Erebus was the father of both Aether and Hemera. Aether represents the bright upper atmosphere, and Hemera the day. Erebus is a word with a rich maritime heritage. The polar explorer Sir James Clark Ross commanded two ships, the EREBUS and the TERROR, on his expedition to Antarctica. These two sister ships would later be trapped in the ice at the other end of the globe in the Arctic. Near King William Island in Victoria Strait they would vanish with all hands on the ill-fated Franklin expedition of 1845, which was looking for the Northwest Passage.

11. After death, deserving classical souls led an afterlife of eternal bliss on the *Islands of the Blest.* These idyllic islands lay somewhere to the west. See the *Oxford Dictionary of Allusions,* p. 198.

12. Information about and images from the Continental Margin Program can be found online in a U.S. Geological Survey report titled *Sea-Floor Photography from the Continental Margin Program* (http://pubs.usgs.gov/of/of01-154/index.htm). The following is a passage from the report's introduction:

"In 1962, Congress authorized the Continental Margin Program, a joint program between the U.S. Geological Survey and the Woods Hole Oceanographic Institution to conduct a geological reconnaissance investigation of the continental shelf and slope off the Atlantic coast of the United States . . . As part of this program approximately 3,800 stations were organized on an 18-kilometer grid that extended from the Canadian border to the southern tip of Florida . . . Bottom photography was conducted at many of these stations in conjunction with sediment sampling for grain size, mineralogy, geochemistry, and biology. The purpose of this report is to release digital versions of these bottom photographs in a gallery that can be visualized geographically."

The ALVIN log quoted in the text, taken from the cruise report for dive 269, is also available online (http://pubs.usgs. gov/of/of01-154/htmldocs/creports/alvin269.htm).

13. Robert Buchsbaum's article "Hiking to Georges Bank" appeared in the July/August 2002 issue of *Sanctuary*, the Massachusetts Audubon Society Magazine (Lincoln, Massachusetts). It is quoted with permission.

14. For more on the natural history of Buzzards Bay, see pp. 19–24 of *Ecology of Buzzards Bay: An Estuarine Profile* by Howes and Goehringer (National Biological Service, Biological Report 31). This very readable report provides an overview of the ecology of Buzzards Bay, that will interest anyone who sails the bay. The report is available in an electronic format (PDF) online (http://www.savebuzzardsbay.org) at the website of the Coalition for Buzzards Bay.

15. The black schooner we saw was probably the SHENANDOAH out of Vineyard Haven, a 108-foot traditional topsail schooner with no engine.

16. For more on the Rubens painting see "Sir Peter Paul—Landscape by Moonlight," an essay by Helen Braham appearing in *The Courtauld Gallery at Somerset House* (1998). She writes: "The Earth, trees and water are bathed in a bright moonlight, the clouds pierced by brilliant stars, represented by dabs of pigment, one a shooting star; the moon and distant trees are

repeated in reflections . . . Rubens achieved this effect of nocturnal solitude only after complex experiment."

The painting is also discussed in *Discourses on Art* by Sir Joshua
Reynolds (edited by Robert R. Wark, 1975): "Rubens has not
only diffused more light over the picture than is in nature, but
has bestowed on it those warm glowing colours by which his
works are so much distinguished."

17. The U.S. National Archives and Records Administration
(NARA) website (http://www.archives.gov/research_room/
genealogy/research_topics/vessel_documents.html) offers a
brief history of vessel documentation, excerpted below:

"Systems for registering and measuring vessels date back to
the English Navigation Laws of Charles II in 1660. These laws
required vessels to be measured and registered to determine
their national character, provide a basis for taxation, and protect
against foreign shipping and shipbuilding. After the American
Revolution, several states adopted the English laws regarding
navigation, but there was no uniformity until the adoption of
the U.S. Constitution. . . . An act of June 7, 1918 (40 Stat. 602),
extended the registration system by requiring the numbering
and recording of every undocumented vessel propelled in whole
or in part by machinery, except vessels under 16 feet using
outboard motors."

For more on the first Congress and vessel documentation,
see *The Birth of the Nation: First Federal Congress 1789 - 1791*, by
Bickford and Bowling (1989), pp. 30–32. George Washington
University also hosts an online exhibit (http://www.gwu.edu/
~ffcp/).

18. To calculate the net tonnage of a boat, multiply one half her
length in feet times her measured beam times her measured depth.
Divide this by 100 and take 90% of the result. In LONDON's case
this is:

$$(27/2) \times 8.5 \times 6.6)/100) \times .90 = 6.81.$$

On LONDON's certificate this seems to have been rounded down to 6 Net Tons.

19. Statistics on the number of Cape Dorys of various sizes built are taken from the California Cape Dory Owners Association website.

20. The Carl Alberg quote appears in "Carl Alberg—His wholesome designs sailed us into the age of fiberglass," by Brian Hill in the February 1984 issue of *Sailing* magazine (Port Washington, Wisconsin: Port Publications, Inc.). See also the Alberg 30 website (http://www.alberg30.org/).

21. Remarks about the Lion's Mane jellyfish are based on *The Atlantic Seashore* by Kenneth L. Gosner (1978, pp. 69–74, 89) and *Sealife* by Geoffrey Waller et al. (1996, p. 96).

22. *The National Audubon Society Field Guide to New England*, by Peter Alden et al., provides an overview of the natural history of New England. If I could only carry one field guide, this would be it. The book offers detailed sections on New England flora, invertebrates, and vertebrates. The central creatures of this book—the Lion's Mane, the osprey, the ocean sunfish—are all listed here. An introductory section also covers New England geography, the weather, and night sky.

23. Arthur Ransome's line about London bookshops can be found in *The Autobiography of Arthur Ransome* (1985, p. 70).

24. Lyrics to the Jimmy Buffett song "Changes in Latitudes, Changes in Attitudes" come from the *Boats, Beaches, Bars & Ballads* box set (Margaritaville/MCA, 1992).

25. Casey and Hackler's remark about Thoreau and cruising can be found on p. xxiii of *Sensible Cruising* (1986).

26. Barbara Hodgson credits a book titled *Lost Islands: The Story of Islands That Have Vanished from Nautical Charts* by Henry Stommel (Vancouver: University of British Columbia Press, 1984) as a source of inspiration for her fascinating graphic novel.

27. Here is a sample post to the Cape Dory Board (http://www.
toolworks.com/capedory/bboard) from April 29, 1999.

> *After a winter of work we are within two weeks of launching* LONDON *(née* LOON*) a 1977 Cape Dory 27, hull # 35. This boat had been out of the water and neglected for ten years.*
>
> *I have only a few remaining questions/problems (special thanks to all the help I have gotten here):*
>
> *1) Every other boat I've sailed with a diesel engine has had some kind of kill switch—usually a knob you pull to kill the engine. My new CD27 has no such device, just an ignition key which the former owner says she just switched off to stop the engine (Yanmar 8). Aren't I in danger of frying some diodes?*
>
> *2) I have the fuel tank out of the boat. I pumped out about seven gallons of foul-looking diesel. It got thicker and dirtier as I got to the bottom. The bottom of the tank looks like the top of a badly burned casserole. I am going to try and get it steam cleaned. Will this be enough or should I chuck it and buy a new one?*
>
> *3) The boat had no anchor light. I have purchased one and the wire. Anyone have a clever way of stringing this through the prone mast? Do I have to take off the masthead to accomplish this? The existing three-strand wire only goes to the lights near the spreader.*
>
> *4) I am having a heck of a time getting the stains off the mast. I have tried all the usual aluminum cleaners—Duro, 3M, Brasso, etc. Any other ideas?*
>
> *5) Finally, there are white vent hoses which lead from an opening behind the engine into the bilge and on up to deck vents to the port and starboard of the lazarette hatch. What are these for? Mine were full of leaves and mice nests and I wonder if they are worth replacing?*
>
> *Thanks again to all for your help and advice.*

28. When I was taught John Masefield's poem "Sea Fever" (1902) at the age of ten, the word "go" was omitted from the first line. This is now thought to be incorrect and the result of a typographical error, and yet I still prefer it: "I must down to the sea again." I was also taught to pronounce "again" in the English manner: *a-gain.*

29. *The Long Way* is Bernard Moitessier's account of his nonstop solo voyage around the world aboard his ketch JOSHUA, ostensibly as a competitor in the first Golden Globe Race (1968–69), which was also written about in the popular account *Voyage For Madmen*. Moitessier laps the globe and is poised to win the race, but during his return through the South Atlantic in March of 1969 he begins to waver from his course north toward Britain and the finish line.

Moitessier finds a mystical sense of peace in being alone with the sea, its creatures, and the sky. It feels so right to him that he continues on, rounds the Cape of Good Hope again, and sails on to his home waters, the Pacific. He writes:

"The wake stretches on and on, white and dense with life by day, luminous by night, like long tresses of dreams and stars. Water runs along the hull and rumbles or sings or rustles, depending on the wind, depending on the sky, depending on whether the sun was setting red or grey . . . Wind, sea, boat and sails, a compact, diffuse whole, without beginning or end, a part and all of the universe . . . my own universe, truly mine."

30. My remarks about Bartholomew Gosnold are based on Harold C. Wilson's book *Gosnold's Hope* (2000, p. 72), which I picked up in the shop at the New Bedford Whaling Museum. This slim volume contains a complete account of Gosnold's expedition to New England and particularly the Elizabeth Islands in 1602—the first complete recorded account of a visit to Buzzards Bay. The author also makes the case that Cuttyhunk, not Bermuda, is the island in Shakespeare's play, *The Tempest*. A chart plots the author's interpretation of Gosnold's route from Provincetown to Buzzards Bay.

Other books of interest:

A SPLENDID MADNESS
A Man • A Boat • A Love Story
by Thomas Froncek

How does a sensible middle-aged family man suddenly find himself clinging to the tiller of a runaway sailboat and shouting for joy? The answers are found in this highly entertaining account of one man's late-blooming love affair with sailing. Froncek's story will stir fond memories among old sailing hands and newcomers alike, will encourage those who dream of someday sailing their own boat, and will enable puzzled friends and family to better understand the strange obsession that grips those who have fallen in love with sailing.

CATBOAT SUMMERS
by John E. Conway

Chronicles a decade's worth of adventure in New England waters through a series of short tales, each recounting one of the Conways' many extraordinary experiences aboard their 100-year-old wooden catboat, BUCKRAMMER. From the hilariously ill-fated participation of a fleet of catboats in Boston Harbor's Sail 2000 Parade to a chilling, phantasmal encounter amidst fog and darkness and even a pilgrimage to the yard where BUCKRAMMER was born, readers will be enthralled by Conway's compelling narrative and whimsical humor.

THE COAST OF SUMMER
Sailing New England Waters from Shelter Island to Cape Cod
by Anthony Bailey

"...an inspired guide in a fascinating locale with a rich past.... Bailey's writing flashes with drollery and wit; he's a comfortable stylist who works on the reader like a masseur." *Kirkus Reviews*
"...an engaging account.... Readers familiar with the area — its shorelines and waters — will savor every word." *Publishers Weekly*

THE COMPLEAT CRUISER
The Art, Practice, and Enjoyment of Boating
by L. Francis Herreshoff

Famed yacht designer and author L. Francis Herreshoff takes readers on family-style cruises in American waters, during which all sorts of boats and boating skills are explained as they are used.
"...delightful..." *Yachting*
"[A] charming classic..." *Next Whole Earth Catalog*

LOGS OF THE DEAD PIRATES SOCIETY
A Schooner Adventure Around Buzzards Bay
by Randall S. Peffer

"...provides vivid descriptions and insights into the Bay's communities and unspoiled coves.... [Peffer] manages to discharge some of man's higher obligations — trying to understand our world well, preserve it, and to educate the next generation — all while living well and smartly." *WoodenBoat*

SHERIDAN HOUSE
America's Favorite Sailing Books
www.sheridanhouse.com